Morning Whispers

Book One:

Daily Journal and Meditations

from the Old Testament

David Morgan

Dedication

It is with love and gratitude that I dedicate this journal to my wife. Betsy has been my companion for forty one years and counting. She has been my constant encourager through the countless adventures the Lord has blessed us with. He knew it was not good for me to be alone so he chose from his entire creation, my one "suitable companion", Betsy.

Introduction

Early each morning, after my talk with the Lord, I sit at my computer, read His word, and listen. This isn't my Bible study time; it's my "listen to what He has to say" time. I've learned over the past 53 years with the Lord that too much talking and thinking can get in the way of listening, especially when He's whispering. As a Marriage and Family Therapist, married to a Marriage and Family Therapist, I'm seldom at a loss for words or conversation, but during those early morning hours, it's my dictation skills, taking not giving, that are most beneficial. Thanks to a boring summer job as an undergraduate many years ago, I learned to type without thinking, so He talks, I listen, and words appear on my computer screen to frequently find their way into my life and therapy sessions throughout the day. The following pages are a few of those morning whispers. His Word is always good; my listening skills are sometimes faulty. I pray that you remember the ones I got right and forget the ones I got wrong.

As you go through this daily journal, I encourage you to read his word and the messages he whispered to me, and then become an active participant. Listen closely to his unique words for you and write them down along with other thoughts, reflections and reactions. Work those messages into your daily life and refer back to them throughout the year as you encounter situations that bring his previous insights to mind.

You'll find a scripture and meditation for every day of the year with a few additional ones included for those days when you need an extra boost to get going. They're called Morning Whispers but feel free to make them your Evening Whispers if that's a better fit for your life. Although you might notice the scriptures are organized according to books of the Bible, there is no particular reason to read them in that order. Go from front to back, back to front, or just open your journal wherever you like and be amazed at how God is able to send just the right message at precisely the right time. It's called his "Living Word" for a reason. If you occasionally need additional space to fully express your thoughts, you'll find it at the back of your journal. Be sure to reference those additional notes with a page number or date. You might find it helpful to date each page as you read and write in your journal. There's an excellent chance you'll begin to see previously unnoticed patterns and plans as you look back and compare dates, events, words from the Lord, and answers to prayers.

Enjoy your journal, enjoy your journey and may God bless you.

David Morgan, M.S., M.F.T.

Job 1:1 *He was honest inside and out, a man of his word, who was totally devoted to God and hated evil with a passion.*

W hat was about to happen to Job was not the result of some secret sin or lack of faith. In the end, God's "perfect will" will be done, but in the meantime bad things happen to good people, good things happen to bad people, good things happen to good people and bad things happen to bad people. Don't spend much time trying to figure that one out, just trust God to help you through whatever happens in your life and know that now or later, in this life or the next, Jesus is the way, the truth, and the life always and forever whether life seems to make sense at the moment or not.

My Reflections and Responses:

_____

_____

_____

_____

_____

_____

_____

Date: _____

Job 1:20-22 *20 Job got to his feet, ripped his robe, shaved his head, then fell to the ground and worshiped: 21 Naked I came from my mother's womb, naked I'll return to the womb of the earth. GOD gives, GOD takes. God's name be ever blessed. 22 Not once through all this did Job sin; not once did he blame God.*

When everything he had was lost, Job worshiped God. Only later, when he tries to understand and make sense out of what is happening, does he get confused, angry, and desperate. Sometimes God gives us a tiny glimpse of a little bit of his plan, but for the most part, we have to live by faith, trust in him, and be obedient, even when we don't understand.

My Reflections and Responses:

_____

_____

_____

_____

_____

_____

_____

_____

Date: _____

Job 2:3 *He still has a firm grip on his integrity!*

Integrity is not Satan's strong suite but God noticed Job's, and pointed it out to Satan. Integrity is only obvious in times of adversity or obscurity. When things are going right, or others are looking, it's much easier to do the right thing. When things are all going wrong, and no one is looking, your attitude and actions expose your integrity.

My Reflections and Responses:

_____

_____

_____

_____

_____

_____

_____

_____

_____

_____

_____

_____

_____

Date: _____   3

Job 2:9 *His wife said, "Still holding on to your precious integrity, are you? Curse God and be done with it!"*

Job's wife didn't understand the meaning of integrity. It's not a tool you use to get what you want; it's made up of and reflective of your core belief about yourself, others and life. It's who you've chosen to be for so long that it becomes who you are; whether, at the moment, it appears to be to your advantage or not is irrelevant.

My Reflections and Responses:

_____

_____

_____

_____

_____

_____

_____

_____

_____

_____

_____

Date: _____

Job 2:10 *He told her, "You're talking like an empty-headed fool. We take the good days from God — why not also the bad days?" Not once through all this did Job sin. He said nothing against God.*

His belief in God and God's goodness made up the very core of his existence and adversity couldn't reach and destroy that.

My Reflections and Responses:

_____

_____

_____

_____

_____

_____

_____

_____

_____

_____

_____

_____

_____

_____

Date: _____   5

Job 2:11-13 *11 Three of Job's friends heard of all the trouble that had fallen on him. Each traveled from his own country — Eliphaz from Teman, Bildad from Shuhah, Zophar from Naamath — and went together to Job to keep him company and comfort him. 13 Then they sat with him on the ground. Seven days and nights they sat there without saying a word. They could see how rotten he felt, how deeply he was suffering.*

What wonderful friends; traveling a long way just to be with a friend and comfort him in his time of need. Job's friends could see how badly he felt and without condemning him, or trying to fix him, they just sat with him and kept him company. If they had just been able to keep their mouths shut, they would have gone down in biblical history as a great example of friendship, but they only lasted seven days. When you've done the right thing, sometimes it's better to just stop before you go on to mess the whole thing up.

My Reflections and Responses:

_____

_____

_____

_____

_____

Date: _____

Job 3:11,20-23 *11 "Why didn't I die at birth, my first breath out of the womb my last? 20 "Why does God bother giving light to the miserable, why bother keeping bitter people alive, 21 Those who want in the worst way to die, and can't, who can't imagine anything better than death, 22 Who count the day of their death and burial the happiest day of their life? 23 What's the point of life when it doesn't make sense, when God blocks all the roads to meaning?*

Before we reach this point, we aren't really aware of how much we need God. We might believe in him and even love him, but we haven't actually understood our need for him. As long as there's the slightest possibility that we might get through life and make sense of it on our own, we're not quite ready to give up our independence and self-reliance. It's only with the realization that, on our own, death is our best friend, that we are really ready to rely on God completely. That's when our new life really begins.

My Reflections and Responses:

_____

_____

_____

_____

_____

_____

Date: _____   7

Job 4:4-6 4 Your words have put stumbling people on their feet, put fresh hope in people about to collapse. 5 But now you're the one in trouble — you're hurting! You've been hit hard and you're reeling from the blow. 6 But shouldn't your devout life give you confidence now? Shouldn't your exemplary life give you hope?

When you've just been crushed and devastated, your life as you've always known it destroyed, the strength and wisdom you've freely given to others in the past is of little comfort. Even a reminder from your so called friends of your past virtuous life does nothing to encourage you. When all hope is gone, you might just need a friend to hope for you until you're able to hope for yourself again. Look for that kind of friend and be that kind of friend.

My Reflections and Responses:

_____

_____

_____

_____

_____

_____

_____

_____

Date: _____   8

Job 6:8-10 8 "All I want is an answer to one prayer, a last request to be honored: 9 Let God step on me — squash me like a bug, and be done with me for good. 10 I'd at least have the satisfaction of not having blasphemed the Holy God, before being pressed past the limits.

Job was so down, discouraged and pushed to the outer limits of his endurance, his only request was for God to kill him quickly before he sinned against God. God had more confidence in Job than Job did. Had God honored Job's last request, think of what Job would have missed out on. Even if you're convinced that death is the only solution left, let God make that decision; you never know what he has in mind, even at the last moment, when all hope is gone.

My Reflections and Responses:

_____

_____

_____

_____

_____

_____

_____

_____

Date: _____   9

Job 6:11-13 *11 Where's the strength to keep my hopes up? What future do I have to keep me going? 12 Do you think I have nerves of steel? Do you think I'm made of iron? 13 Do you think I can pull myself up by my bootstraps? Why, I don't even have any boots!*

When you have no strength, no resources, and no hope of ever having any, the only thing left is stupid faith and blind obedience. Stupid faith is faith that makes no earthly sense and blind obedience is just doing what you're told with absolutely no understand of why. That's the exact moment that God will do what only God can do because you've finally gotten out of the way.

My Reflections and Responses:

_____

_____

_____

_____

_____

_____

_____

_____

_____

Date: _____   10

Job 6:24-27 24 *"Confront me with the truth and I'll shut up, show me where I've gone off the track. 25 Honest words never hurt anyone, but what's the point of all this pious bluster? 26 You pretend to tell me what's wrong with my life, but treat my words of anguish as so much hot air. 27 Are people mere things to you? Are friends just items of profit and loss?*

Job's friends didn't really listen to what he was saying. He didn't need to be told all the things he already knew were true but were of no comfort at a time when his whole world had been turned upside-down. He wasn't asking for anything except someone to listen and care about what he was going through and how he was feeling. His friends were too busy telling him what he was doing wrong and how to fix it to just be there for him. When someone comes to you with a problem, really listen and find out what they're asking before you offer them a quick fix.

My Reflections and Responses:

_____

_____

_____

_____

_____

_____

Date: _____

Job 7:1 *"Human life is a struggle, isn't it? It's a life sentence to hard labor.*

When nothing seems to be going right, you can grieve over the loss of what was and become discouraged, or use that memory of better times to encourage you and give you hope for a better future than what you're going through at the moment. When you're doing hard time, don't forget God's promise; you will go through plenty of good times and bad times but he will be with you at all times.

My Reflections and Responses:

_____

_____

_____

_____

_____

_____

_____

_____

_____

_____

Date: _____   12

Job 7:11-16 *11 "And so I'm not keeping one bit of this quiet, I'm laying it all out on the table; my complaining to high heaven is bitter, but honest. 12 Are you going to put a muzzle on me, the way you quiet the sea and still the storm? 13 If I say, 'I'm going to bed, then I'll feel better. A little nap will lift my spirits,' 14 You come and so scare me with nightmares and frighten me with ghosts 15 That I'd rather strangle in the bedclothes than face this kind of life any longer. 16 I hate this life! Who needs any more of this? Let me alone! There's nothing to my life — it's nothing but smoke.*

Job wasn't afraid to tell God what he really thought; don't you be. Job might not have always gotten the facts right, but he was honest with God about how he felt. Follow Job's example. God can handle the tough questions. He always has an answer; sometimes he'll explain, sometimes he won't, but even if he doesn't, he's not playing games; he's just protecting you from what you're not ready to know.

My Reflections and Responses:

_____

_____

_____

_____

_____

_____

Job 7:19-21 *19 Let up on me, will you? Can't you even let me spit in peace? 20 Even suppose I'd sinned — how would that hurt you? You're responsible for every human being. Don't you have better things to do than pick on me? Why make a federal case out of me? 21 Why don't you just forgive my sins and start me off with a clean slate? The way things are going, I'll soon be dead. You'll look high and low, but I won't be around."*

God always sees the big picture; Job didn't and you can't. You can ask for clarification, seek an explanation, offer a recommendation, but if, in the end, you put your trust in God, he'll make the right call every time.

My Reflections and Responses:

_____

_____

_____

_____

_____

_____

_____

_____

_____

Date: _____   14

Job 8:2-20 *2 "How can you keep on talking like this? You're talking nonsense, and noisy nonsense at that. 3 Does God mess up? Does God Almighty ever get things backwards? 4 It's plain that your children sinned against him — otherwise, why would God have punished them? 5 Here's what you must do — and don't put it off any longer: Get down on your knees before God Almighty. 6 If you're as innocent and upright as you say, it's not too late — he'll come running; he'll set everything right again, reestablish your fortunes. 7 Even though you're not much right now, you'll end up better than ever. 20 "There's no way that God will reject a good person, and there is no way he'll help a bad one.*

Job's friends couldn't believe he would talk to God like that; that's because Job knew God, his friends knew about God. They got some of their facts right but didn't really understand Job or God. Yes God would restore Job. No, God wouldn't come running; he didn't need to, he was already there. No, God doesn't reject people on the basis of their being good or bad; they accept or reject him. Yes, God will help bad people; no one is good enough to deserve his help anyway, he does it because of his goodness, not theirs.

My Reflections and Responses:

_____

_____

_____

_____

Date: _____   15

Job 9:1-4 *1 Job continued by saying: 2 "So what's new? I know all this. The question is, 'How can mere mortals get right with God?' 3 If we wanted to bring our case before him, what chance would we have? Not one in a thousand! 4 God's wisdom is so deep, God's power so immense, who could take him on and come out in one piece?*

The question has always been, "How can mere mortals get right with God?" The answer has always been, "We can't." God is the one who makes us right with him; he's the one who saves us, we can't save ourselves. Even if it were possible to achieve perfection, that perfection would only reflect Gods creative power, not ours. We will always and only be the created, not the creator. That's not a bad thing; we just have to accept that our purpose is to love and be loved, not to be the boss. All the trouble on earth started when Adam and Eve decided it wasn't enough to be loved by God; they wanted to be like God, so they ate from the tree of the knowledge of good and evil, and the rest is history.

My Reflections and Responses:

_____

_____

_____

_____

_____

Date: _____   16

Job 9:10-11 *10 We'll never comprehend all the great things he does; his miracle-surprises can't be counted. 11 Somehow, though he moves right in front of me, I don't see him; quietly but surely he's active, and I miss it.*

X-rays pass right through our bodies and we'd never know it if the image wasn't captured on film; we can't see, touch, taste or feel them. God sometimes gives us a little glimpse of himself through his creation. Like the X-rays, he passes through us, walks among us, and does what he does without our knowledge. Once in a while he shows us the film, a brief look at the results of his having been here; most of the time we live our lives benefiting from but unaware of his ever presence. We'll never comprehend him but the closer we pay attention, the more aware we will become of him.

My Reflections and Responses:

_____

_____

_____

_____

_____

_____

_____

Date: _____

Job 9:23-24 *23 When calamity hits and brings sudden death, he folds his arms, aloof from the despair of the innocent. 24 He lets the wicked take over running the world, he installs judges who can't tell right from wrong. If he's not responsible, who is?*

While it's true that nothing in this world happens without God's permission, it's not true that he causes everything that happens. We're good at making a mess without asking for his help, but quick to blame him for it when things don't work out the way we anticipated. We vote for ungodly officials, who appoint judges who can't tell right from wrong, or worse yet, we don't vote at all, and then blame God for the results. To answer Job's question, "If he's not responsible, who is?" we are. Thank God he doesn't leave us with the mess of our own making. If we turn to him and trust in him, he will turn our disasters into experience and wisdom for our future benefit.

My Reflections and Responses:

_____

_____

_____

_____

_____

_____

Date: _____   18

Job 10:1 *"I can't stand my life — I hate it! I'm putting it all out on the table, all the bitterness of my life — I'm holding back nothing."*

G od is waiting for us to get to the point where we hate our lives, and are willing to hold back nothing; that's when he can give us maybe not everything we want, but everything we need for an abundant life with him.

My Reflections and Responses:

_____

_____

_____

_____

_____

_____

_____

_____

_____

_____

_____

Date: _____

Job 10:8-9 8 *"You made me like a handcrafted piece of pottery — and now are you going to smash me to pieces? 9 Don't you remember how beautifully you worked my clay? Will you reduce me now to a mud pie?*

For a little while, Job forgot that no matter how beautifully made, the pottery's real glory and purpose is in what it contains. God allowed the container to be battered and beaten, but the contents, Job's essence, his sole and spirit, were off limits to the enemy. Even a mud pie can be a beautiful thing if it contains God's favorite creation, us.

My Reflections and Responses:

_____

_____

_____

_____

_____

_____

_____

_____

_____

_____

Date: _____   20

Job 11:11-12 *11 He sees through vain pretensions, spots evil a long way off — no one pulls the wool over his eyes! 12 Hollow men, hollow women, will wise up about the same time mules learn to talk.*

Once again, Job's "so called friends" couldn't stop drawing conclusions about what was taking place on the inside, based on what was happening on the outside. They assumed that everything bad that happened to Job was a direct result of his sin. Sometimes bad things happen to good people and good things happen to bad people. That fact alone should make us very cautious about making judgments concerning the condition of people's hearts based on outward appearances. As for why this happens, only God really knows.

My Reflections and Responses:

_____

_____

_____

_____

_____

_____

_____

_____

_____

Date: _____

Job 12:1-3 *1 Job answered: 2 "I'm sure you speak for all the experts, and when you die there'll be no one left to tell us how to live. 3 But don't forget that I also have a brain — I don't intend to play second fiddle to you. It doesn't take an expert to know these things.*

Job's friends were heavy on the information but totally lacking in the understanding department. Often our discouragement is not based on a lack of information, we know the right answer; it's a lack of inspiration and difficulty with the application that gets us down. We don't need someone to tell us what to do; we need someone to care about what we are going through and give us a little encouragement. We need someone to believe in us when we are having a hard time believing for our self.

My Reflections and Responses:

_____

_____

_____

_____

_____

_____

_____

Date: _____   22

Job 12:4 *"I'm ridiculed by my friends: 'So that's the man who had conversations with God!' Ridiculed without mercy: 'Look at the man who never did wrong!'*

When you live a life so connected to God that the two of you talk, you're living on a higher level than those around you, even your friends. This doesn't make you better than others, although they might think you think it does; it just means you're walking with God, in touch with his will for your life, and submitted to his way. There will be some who can't wait to see you fall; catch you in some sin, not out of meanness, but because of their own self imposed feelings of inferiority and insecurity. If you fail, they don't feel so bad about their own shortcomings. Try to understand where they're coming from and don't let them get you down. Don't get down on yourself either, because you weren't perfect; God never expected or intended for you to be perfect, if he had, he'd have made you with no flaws and probably no brain.

My Reflections and Responses:

_____

_____

_____

_____

Date: _____

Job 12:12-13 *12 Do you think the elderly have a corner on wisdom, that you have to grow old before you understand life? 13 "True wisdom and real power belong to God; from him we learn how to live, and also what to live for.*

Sometimes it takes a long time for us to get it, that true wisdom and real power belong to God, and we end up old before we finally understand, but it wasn't old age that made us wise. God's wisdom can come at any age; understanding life will happen when we start listening to the one who created it.

My Reflections and Responses:

_____

_____

_____

_____

_____

_____

_____

_____

_____

_____

Date: _____   24

Job 13:1-5 *1 "Yes, I've seen all this with my own eyes, heard and understood it with my very own ears. 2 Everything you know, I know, so I'm not taking a back seat to any of you. 3 I'm taking my case straight to God Almighty; I've had it with you — I'm going directly to God. 4 You graffiti my life with lies. You're a bunch of pompous quacks! 5 I wish you'd shut your mouths — silence is your only claim to wisdom.*

Job acknowledges the accuracy of their information when he says he knows everything they know, and yet he calls them lying, pompous quacks. Truth is more than accurate information, and wisdom is more than understanding. Wisdom and truth include the application of information and understanding in the spirit of love; otherwise it's just using bits and pieces of the truth to tell a lie.

My Reflections and Responses:

_____

_____

_____

_____

_____

_____

_____

_____

Date: _____   25

Job 13:6-8 *6 "Listen now while I make my case, consider my side of things for a change. 7 Or are you going to keep on lying 'to do God a service'? to make up stories 'to get him off the hook'? 8 Why do you always take his side? Do you think he needs a lawyer to defend himself?*

To defend God reveals a lack of trust in him. Defending him assumes that he can and needs to be understood and explained. If someone, out of their hurt and confusion, is angry with God, try listening to and understanding them. You are God's hand here on earth for those who are having a difficult time reaching him directly. It's not your job to defend God but to allow him to love them through you. When God is really known, he doesn't need to be explained.

My Reflections and Responses:

_____

_____

_____

_____

_____

_____

_____

_____

Date: _____   26

Job 13:12 *Your wise sayings are knickknack wisdom, good for nothing but gathering dust.*

Wise sayings that are memorized or even made up on the spot for the occasion, but aren't the result of listening, understanding, and speaking God's revealed truth in love, don't instruct or restore; they're just a collection of poetry and prose, recited to impress others and make the speaker feel better, but do nothing for the person who is in need of help.

My Reflections and Responses:

_____

_____

_____

_____

_____

_____

_____

_____

_____

_____

_____

Date: _____   27

Job 13:20-22 *20 "Please, God, I have two requests; grant them so I'll know I count with you: 21 First, lay off the afflictions; the terror is too much for me. 22 Second, address me directly so I can answer you, or let me speak and then you answer me.*

Job never lost his belief in God but he felt abandoned and lost the feeling of being connected, watched over and protected by God. When God stopped speaking, Job started vacillating between his feelings of despair and his knowledge of God's true nature. When we stop feeling or sensing God's presence, and have to rely only on our knowledge and faith, it's easy to lose hope and start doubting the very things we've come to know and believe in. Feeling separated from God doesn't mean being separated from him. That's when faith is hardened into steel or abandoned altogether. God will allow the feelings to return, but he might wait long enough for us to learn not to rely on them.

My Reflections and Responses:

_____

_____

_____

_____

_____

_____

Date: _____   28

Job 15:2-5 2 *"If you were truly wise, would you sound so much like a windbag, belching hot air? 3 Would you talk nonsense in the middle of a serious argument, babbling baloney? 4 Look at you! You trivialize religion, turn spiritual conversation into empty gossip. 5 It's your sin that taught you to talk this way.*

Job was pouring his heart out to God and his friends were making fun of him, putting him down, and condemning him for his feelings of frustration and confusion. Job threw out all the rules of etiquette and was getting real with God; his friends, having never had a close up and personal relationship with God, mistook this honesty for nonsense and would have preferred a much more formal and polite conversation with him. Take your lesson from Job, not his friends; drop all pretenses and just get real with God; he won't be offended, and you won't be rejected.

My Reflections and Responses:

_____

_____

_____

_____

_____

_____

Date: _____   29

Job 15:7-10 *7 Do you think you're the first person to have to deal with these things? Have you been around as long as the hills? 8 Were you listening in when God planned all this? Do you think you're the only one who knows anything? 9 What do you know that we don't know? What insights do you have that we've missed? 10 Gray beards and white hair back us up —old folks who've been around a lot longer than you.*

Job's "old" friends thought being old made them smart; it just gave them more time to be dumb. They wanted to know what Job thought he knew that they didn't already know and completely missed the point; it wasn't what Job knew but who he knew in a very personal way, God. They knew all about God, Job knew God; that's why he was so distraught and confused when God stopped talking to him in a way that he had become so familiar with.

My Reflections and Responses:

_____

_____

_____

_____

_____

_____

_____

Date: _____   30

Job 16:2-5 *2 "I've had all I can take of your talk. What a bunch of miserable comforters! 3 Is there no end to your windbag speeches? What's your problem that you go on and on like this? 4 If you were in my shoes, I could talk just like you. I could put together a terrific harangue and really let you have it. 5 But I'd never do that. I'd console and comfort, make things better, not worse!*

B e the kind of friend Job said he would be. When your friend is going through a terrible time, just be with him to console and comfort him. Later on, if he asks, you can share your insights and ideas, but what he really needs now is your comforting presence and assurance that he's not alone; anything more is really less.

My Reflections and Responses:

_____

_____

_____

_____

_____

_____

_____

_____

_____

Date: _____   31

Job 17:1-2 *"My spirit is broken, my days used up, my grave dug and waiting. 2 See how these mockers close in on me? How long do I have to put up with their insolence?*

Don't call it quits until God pulls the plug. You never know what he has for you tomorrow, next week, or maybe next year. Look what Job would have given up if he had taken matters into his own hands and ended it all right there. If life was easy, you'd handle it yourself; if it was difficult, you'd get help from your friends. It's because life is sometimes impossible that you need God; he specializes in the impossible.

My Reflections and Responses:

_____

_____

_____

_____

_____

_____

_____

_____

_____

Date: _____   32

Job 17:10 *"Maybe you'd all like to start over, to try it again, the bunch of you. So far I haven't come across one scrap of wisdom in anything you've said.*

Job sarcastically asked his friends to try a different approach. They were throwing around plenty of information but he could find no wisdom in it. If your friends mess up in their attempt to be there for you in your time of need, tell them what you really need and give them a chance to try again; you might want to leave out the sarcasm.

My Reflections and Responses:

_____

_____

_____

_____

_____

_____

_____

_____

_____

_____

Date: _____   33

Job 18:5-6 5 *"Here's the rule: The light of the wicked is put out. Their flame dies down and is extinguished. 6 Their house goes dark — every lamp in the place goes out.*

One of the problems of trying to live life by a rigid set of rules is that you end up applying the rules to everything, whether they fit or not. The rules become more important than the people they are made to protect. If the rule is "bad things happen to bad people", then everyone who's ever had something bad happen to them must be bad. What if something bad happens to a good person? It doesn't follow the rule so it's not possible; it's either not really a bad thing or the person is really bad but we just didn't realize it. Everyone ends up being judged by their circumstance or current situation, not the condition of their heart.

My Reflections and Responses:

_____

_____

_____

_____

_____

_____

_____

Date: _____   34

Job 19:1-5 *1 Job answered: 2 "How long are you going to keep battering away at me, pounding me with these harangues? 3 Time after time after time you jump all over me. Do you have no conscience, abusing me like this? 4 Even if I have, somehow or other, gotten off the track, what business is that of yours? 5 Why do you insist on putting me down, using my troubles as a stick to beat me?*

Job's friends used his situation as proof that he was evil and deserved to be punished. The possibility that Job might be innocent didn't fit into their book of rules or God concept so they didn't even consider it. The possibility that Job might be guilty but still be in need of compassion and understanding instead of judgment, didn't fit their rigid way of thinking, so it never occurred to them.

My Reflections and Responses:

_____

_____

_____

_____

_____

_____

_____

_____

Date: _____   35

Job 19:13-15 *13 "God alienated my family from me; 14 everyone who knows me avoids me. My relatives and friends have all left; houseguests forget I ever existed. 15 The servant girls treat me like a bum off the street, look at me like they've never seen me before.*

Although Job mistakenly attributed his situation to God, not Satan, he was learning a harsh reality about people; when you're a success, everyone is your friend. When you've lost everything, it's hard to find anyone who remembers you. Be the rare individual who remembers a person by name, not by their success.

My Reflections and Responses:

_____

_____

_____

_____

_____

_____

_____

_____

_____

_____

_____

Date: _____

Job 19:21-22 21 *"Oh, friends, dear friends, take pity on me. God has come down hard on me! 22 Do you have to be hard on me too? Don't you ever tire of abusing me?*

Y ou teach your children to look both ways, but if they walk out into the street without looking, and get hit by a truck, you don't really care if it was their own fault; you rush to them, take care of their injuries, and comfort them. Your heart is broken because the one you love is hurting; nothing else matters at the moment.

My Reflections and Responses:

_____

_____

_____

_____

_____

_____

_____

_____

_____

_____

_____

Job 19:25-27 *25 Still, I know that God lives — the One who gives me back my life — and eventually he'll take his stand on earth. 26 And I'll see him — even though I get skinned alive! — 27 see God myself, with my very own eyes. Oh, how I long for that day!*

Job knew God so well and trusted him so much that when he experienced something totally beyond his comprehension, completely at odds with what he understood about God's ways, he still believed in God and his goodness. Nothing, not even death, could shake that belief. His faith was not dependent upon his understanding.

My Reflections and Responses:

_____

_____

_____

_____

_____

_____

_____

_____

_____

_____

Date: _____   38

Job 19:28-29 28 *"If you're thinking, 'How can we get through to him, get him to see that his trouble is all his own fault?' 29 Forget it. Start worrying about yourselves. Worry about your own sins and God's coming judgment, for judgment is most certainly on the way."*

Don't blame God for every bad thing that happens. Don't blame others for every misfortune they experience; finally, don't blame yourself for everything that goes wrong in your life. The Christian life isn't about blame or guilt; there will always be plenty of that to go around if that's what you're focused on. The Christian life is about getting beyond all of that; it's about forgiveness, restoration, grace and living an abundant if somewhat imperfect life thanks to the one who made it all possible, Jesus.

My Reflections and Responses:

_____

_____

_____

_____

_____

_____

_____

Date: _____

Job 20:3-7 *3 How dare you insult my intelligence like this! Well, here's a piece of my mind! 4 "Don't you even know the basics, how things have been since the earliest days, when Adam and Eve were first placed on earth? 5 The good times of the wicked are short-lived; godless joy is only momentary. 6 The evil might become world famous, strutting at the head of the celebrity parade, 7 But still end up in a pile of dung.*

It would be so easy to have faith if everything just made sense; the good rewarded, the bad punished. While that will eventually all get sorted out in Heaven, here on planet earth, things are a mess. What goes on down here often make no sense at all, is totally beyond our comprehension, and is frequently left in an unresolved, unsatisfactory state. That's when faith is essential, not optional; when knowing God so personally and intimately allows us to trust and obey without understanding.

My Reflections and Responses:

_____

_____

_____

_____

_____

_____

Date: _____   40

Job 21:1-5 1 Job replied: 2 "Now listen to me carefully, please listen, at least do me the favor of listening. 3 Put up with me while I have my say — then you can mock me later to your heart's content. 4 "It's not you I'm complaining to — it's God. Is it any wonder I'm getting fed up with his silence? 5 Take a good look at me. Aren't you appalled by what's happened? No! Don't say anything. I can do without your comments.

Job wasn't complaining to his friends, he wasn't asking them to fix things, he just wanted to be listened to; he needed a little moral support in his time of difficulty and confusion. Realizing that he wasn't likely to get what he needed from them, he asked them not to say anything.

My Reflections and Responses:

_____

_____

_____

_____

_____

_____

_____

_____

_____

Date: _____

Job 21:17-21 17 *"Still, how often does it happen that the wicked fail, or disaster strikes, or they get their just deserts? 18 How often are they blown away by bad luck? Not very often. 19 You might say, 'God is saving up the punishment for their children.' I say, 'Give it to them right now so they'll know what they've done!' 20 They deserve to experience the effects of their evil, feel the full force of God's wrath firsthand. 21 What do they care what happens to their families after they're safely tucked away in the grave?*

Things weren't going according to Job's sense of justice. He was trying to make sense out of what was happening but couldn't come up with an adequate explanation. How often have you tried to explain or understand God and come up short? Sometimes, later on, it all comes together and what appeared to make no sense, now does; sometimes it never does. Quite often we have to rely on the knowledge that he is God, knows what he's doing, will be there for us regardless of the circumstance, drop it and just move on.

My Reflections and Responses:

_____

_____

_____

_____

_____

Date: _____

Job 21:22-26 *22 "But who are we to tell God how to run his affairs? He's dealing with matters that are way over our heads. 23 Some people die in the prime of life, with everything going for them — 24 fat and sassy. 25 Others die bitter and bereft, never getting a taste of happiness. 26 They're laid out side by side in the cemetery, where the worms can't tell one from the other.*

Finally Job came back to the understanding that he didn't need to understand. If we only trusted God with what we could understand, we wouldn't need to trust him at all. Sometimes it's a relief to turn everything over to him without even trying to understand it all; at other times, when things aren't going the way we would very much like, it's extremely frustrating; at all times trusting in him is the right thing to do.

My Reflections and Responses:

_____

_____

_____

_____

_____

_____

_____

_____

Date: _____   43

Job 22:3-6 3 So what if you were righteous — would God Almighty even notice? Even if you gave a perfect performance, do you think he'd applaud? 4 Do you think it's because he cares about your purity that he's disciplining you, putting you on the spot? 5 Hardly! It's because you're a first-class moral failure, because there's no end to your sins. 6 When people came to you for help, you took the shirts off their backs, exploited their helplessness.

Job's friends rewrote history to fit their ideas of justice. They judged Job to be a moral failure because that was the only explanation they could come up with to justify in their own minds what he was going through. Actually, God did and does notice Job and every one of us. He is concerned with every aspect of our lives down to the very number of hairs on our heads. Going through a difficult time doesn't mean that God isn't paying attention. He's always there and always cares. He doesn't always micromanage our lives; it pleases him to give us tremendous freedom to explore our world without worrying all the time about offending him. Keep to his principles, the most important being to love him and love others, and enjoy that freedom.

My Reflections and Responses:

_____

_____

_____

Date: _____   44

Job 22:21-25 21 *"Give in to God, come to terms with him and everything will turn out just fine. 22 Let him tell you what to do; take his words to heart. 23 Come back to God Almighty and he'll rebuild your life. Clean house of everything evil. 24 Relax your grip on your money and abandon your gold-plated luxury. 25 God Almighty will be your treasure, more wealth than you can imagine.*

P retty good advice if Job had done all those things. God would have brought him back if he'd ever strayed in the first place, but what if he or you haven't strayed; you've done everything you know to do? What if you've repented of every sin, honored God in every way and lived the best life you know how to live and it seems to be falling apart anyway? Walking with God doesn't mean you get to avoid the mess that man and the enemy have made of this world; it means that you don't have to walk through it alone. Don't spend too much time trying to explain or understand it; trust that God will somehow get you through it and will use even the bad experiences in your life, whether of your own making or not, for your ultimate good.

My Reflections and Responses:

_____

_____

_____

Date: _____   45

Job 23:1-7 *1 Job replied: 2 "I'm not letting up — I'm standing my ground. My complaint is legitimate. God has no right to treat me like this — it isn't fair! 3 If I knew where on earth to find him, I'd go straight to him. 4 I'd lay my case before him face-to-face, give him all my arguments firsthand. 5 I'd find out exactly what he's thinking, discover what's going on in his head. 6 Do you think he'd dismiss me or bully me? No, he'd take me seriously. 7 He'd see a straight-living man standing before him; my Judge would acquit me for good of all charges.*

Even when things are really bad, when live is completely unfair, hang on to the belief that Job had that God would not dismiss him but take him seriously if he could just have a word with him. Job didn't know everything that God knew, and we don't either. If we knew everything that God knows, we would understand everything that God does or allows, but trying to be as smart as God was the worst mistake Adam and Eve ever made for themselves and everyone that followed. Let God be God and trust that he knows what he's doing, even when you don't.

My Reflections and Responses:

_____

_____

_____

_____

Date: _____   46

Job 23:11-12 *11 I've followed him closely, my feet in his footprints, not once swerving from his way. 12 I've obeyed every word he's spoken, and not just obeyed his advice — I've treasured it.*

Job examined his whole live, looking for cause and effect in what was happening to him. His friends' way of thinking was starting to affect him.

My Reflections and Responses:

_____

_____

_____

_____

_____

_____

_____

_____

_____

_____

_____

_____

_____

Date: _____   47

Job 24:12 *People are dying right and left, groaning in torment. The wretched cry out for help and God does nothing, acts like nothing's wrong!*

Have you ever asked "where is God when you really need him"? Have you ever asked, "what kind of god would allow this to happen"? Have you insisted on trusting and loving him even without a satisfactory answer? You're beginning to understand real faith.

My Reflections and Responses:

_____

_____

_____

_____

_____

_____

_____

_____

_____

_____

_____

Date: _____   48

Job 24:13-17 13 *"Then there are those who avoid light at all costs, who scorn the light-filled path. 14 When the sun goes down, the murderer gets up — kills the poor and robs the defenseless. 15 Sexual predators can't wait for nightfall, thinking, 'No one can see us now.' 16 Burglars do their work at night, but keep well out of sight through the day. They want nothing to do with light. 17 Deep darkness is morning for that bunch; they make the terrors of darkness their companions in crime.*

Job was being exposed to the evils of this world in a totally new way and it wasn't adding up. Have you ever seen something so unfair that it made you question God's plan and his methods? You're in good company.

My Reflections and Responses:

_____

_____

_____

_____

_____

_____

_____

_____

_____

Date: _____   49

Job 25:2-6 *2 "God is sovereign, God is fearsome — everything in the cosmos fits and works in his plan. 3 Can anyone count his angel armies? Is there any place where his light doesn't shine? 4 How can a mere mortal presume to stand up to God? How can an ordinary person pretend to be guiltless? 5 Why, even the moon has its flaws, even the stars aren't perfect in God's eyes, 6 So how much less, plain men and women — slugs and maggots by comparison!"*

Job's friends had a pretty poor opinion of God's favorite creation, man. They must have thought that perfect was preferred, not understanding that God could have made us that way if he'd wanted. It's in our imperfection that God takes delight. A perfect creature would have no need for relationship or for a savior; it would be self-sufficient. God's perfect plan required imperfect people who would love and need and want a relationship with him.

My Reflections and Responses:

_____

_____

_____

_____

_____

_____

Date: _____   50

Job 26:2-4 2 "Well, you've certainly been a great help to a helpless man! You came to the rescue just in the nick of time! 3 What wonderful advice you've given to a mixed-up man! What amazing insights you've provided! 4 Where in the world did you learn all this? How did you become so inspired?

Job, even in his darkest hour, was wise enough to spot a phony. He realized the help he was offered was no help at all. Had he accepted his friends' tirades as genuine wisdom, he would have been in more trouble than he already was. They weren't well-meaning, they were self-righteous, and their advice had no real application except to make themselves feel superior. Even when you're desperate and reaching out for any help you can find, make sure it's worth accepting; the wrong kind of help is worse than no help at all.

My Reflections and Responses:

_____

_____

_____

_____

_____

_____

_____

Job 28:20-28 20 *"So where does Wisdom come from? And where does Insight live? 21 It can't be found by looking, no matter how deep you dig, no matter how high you fly. 22 If you search through the graveyard and question the dead, they say, 'We've only heard rumors of it.' 23 "God alone knows the way to Wisdom, he knows the exact place to find it. 24 He knows where everything is on earth, he sees everything under heaven. 25 After he commanded the winds to blow and measured out the waters, 26 Arranged for the rain and set off explosions of thunder and lightning, 27 He focused on Wisdom, made sure it was all set and tested and ready. 28 Then he addressed the human race: 'Here it is! Fear-of-the-Lord — that's Wisdom, and Insight means shunning evil.'"*

Knowledge is acquired, wisdom is bestowed. You can accumulate as much knowledge and information as you like but it doesn't mean you'll know what to do with it once you have it. Knowledge without wisdom is like a tool in the hands of an unskilled worker; someone will eventually end up getting hurt. You can't find it, learn it or earn it; if you really want wisdom, submit yourself completely to the Lord; he's the only one handing it out and he's extremely generous.

My Reflections and Responses:

_____

_____

_____

_____

Date: _____   52

Job 29:2-6 2 "Oh, how I long for the good old days, when God took such very good care of me. 3 He always held a lamp before me and I walked through the dark by its light. 4 Oh, how I miss those golden years when God's friendship graced my home, 5 When the Mighty One was still by my side and my children were all around me, 6 When everything was going my way, and nothing seemed too difficult.

Job's response to the cruelty and unfairness of life continues through the next three chapters. Job, the best of the best, was totally overwhelmed; his understanding of good and evil, reward and punishment, fair and unfair completely destroyed. What more could you expect from any man who'd been put through the torment Job suffered? This is just a glimpse of what one man, Jesus, volunteered to go through out of love for us.

My Reflections and Responses:

_____

_____

_____

_____

_____

_____

_____

_____

Date: _____   53

Job 32:6-10 *6 "I'm a young man, and you are all old and experienced. That's why I kept quiet and held back from joining the discussion. 7 I kept thinking, 'Experience will tell. The longer you live, the wiser you become.' 8 But I see I was wrong — it's God's Spirit in a person, the breath of the Almighty One, that makes wise human insight possible. 9 The experts have no corner on wisdom; getting old doesn't guarantee good sense. 10 So I've decided to speak up. Listen well! I'm going to tell you exactly what I think.*

Job's youngest friend finally came to realize that wisdom isn't a function of experience, age, informa-tion or knowledge; it's God's Spirit in a person. If wisdom is actually a person, God's Spirit, not a thing, it's God with us and in us that allows his wisdom to flow through us. Since Jesus sent his Spirit to fill us and live in us, his wisdom is available to us at all times; we just have to get out of the way and allow it to operate in us.

My Reflections and Responses:

_____

_____

_____

_____

_____

_____

_____

Date: _____   54

Job 33:8 *"Here's what you said. I heard you say it with my own ears.*

Job's youngest friend was the only one who respected him enough to actually listened and hear what he was saying. The others were so anxious to jump in with their instant solutions, they tried to answer questions that weren't even asked and give help that wasn't even wanted.

My Reflections and Responses:

_____

_____

_____

_____

_____

_____

_____

_____

_____

_____

_____

_____

Date: _____   55

Job 37:14-18 *14 "Job, are you listening? Have you noticed all this? Stop in your tracks! Take in God's miracle-wonders! 15 Do you have any idea how God does it all, how he makes bright lightning from dark storms, 16 How he piles up the cumulus clouds — all these miracle-wonders of a perfect Mind? 17 Why, you don't even know how to keep cool on a sweltering hot day, 18 So how could you even dream of making a dent in that hot-tin-roof sky?*

If we would just stop for a moment and pay attention to the enormity and majesty of God's creation, we would never panic; he put together such a vast universe with marvelous precision, paying so close attention to each minute detail, that we couldn't help conclude that he is fully capable and willing to take care of our every need. He made us and knows what needs fixing even before it breaks.

My Reflections and Responses:

_____

_____

_____

_____

_____

_____

_____

Date: _____

Job 37:23-24   *23 "Mighty God! Far beyond our reach! Unsurpassable in power and justice! It's unthinkable that he'd treat anyone unfairly. 24 So bow to him in deep reverence, one and all! If you're wise, you'll most certainly worship him."*

It is unthinkable that God would treat anyone unfairly. Because he is God, everything he does is automatically the right thing. That God is unloving, unkind, unjust or just wrong, will never be the correct explanation to any question. If you're looking for an answer, and one explanation can never be right, you need to keep looking or start trusting.

My Reflections and Responses:

_____

_____

_____

_____

_____

_____

_____

_____

_____

_____

Date: _____

Job 38:1-4 *1 And now, finally, GOD answered Job from the eye of a violent storm. He said: 2 "Why do you confuse the issue? Why do you talk without knowing what you're talking about? 3 Pull yourself together, Job! Up on your feet! Stand tall! I have some questions for you, and I want some straight answers. 4 Where were you when I created the earth? Tell me, since you know so much!*

This was the first of many questions that Job couldn't begin to answer; actually, he couldn't answer any of God's questions. Job didn't even know enough to ask the right questions.

My Reflections and Responses:

_____

_____

_____

_____

_____

_____

_____

_____

_____

_____

_____

Date: _____

Job 40:1-2 *1 GOD then confronted Job directly: 2 "Now what do you have to say for yourself? Are you going to haul me, the Mighty One, into court and press charges?"*

Have you ever gone on and on, complaining about someone and then turned around to find that they'd been right there all along, listening to every word? Job made the mistake of assuming that God wasn't listening just because he wasn't talking. When God decided to speak, Job became painfully aware that God had been there from the beginning, not the beginning of Job's troubles, the beginning of time. God had a perfect plan all along, had never lost sight of his friend Job and what he was going through, but felt no obligation to let Job in on his plan until the moment of his choosing. God will not be rushed, but he will never be late. You can try to speed things up, but you'll only succeed in frustrating yourself. Why bother?

My Reflections and Responses:

_____

_____

_____

_____

_____

Date: _____

Job 40:3-5 *3 I'm Ready to Shut Up and Listen Job answered: 4 "I'm speechless, in awe — words fail me. I should never have opened my mouth! 5 I've talked too much, way too much. I'm ready to shut up and listen."*

Job said he was speechless but managed to say a few more things before he finally shut up and listened. Sometimes the hardest thing to do or say is nothing.

My Reflections and Responses:

_____

_____

_____

_____

_____

_____

_____

_____

_____

_____

_____

Date: _____   60

Job 40:6–8 *6 GOD addressed Job next from the eye of the storm, and this is what he said: 7 "I have some more questions for you, and I want straight answers. 8 "Do you presume to tell me what I'm doing wrong?*

God wasn't quite ready to let Job off the hook. He wanted Job and us to learn from Job's mistakes. They had been friends for so long that Job almost forgot which one was God and which one was man. He was beginning to get the picture. God wants us to come to him with anything and everything, but to always remember who's who.

My Reflections and Responses:

_____

_____

_____

_____

_____

_____

_____

_____

_____

_____

Date: _____   61

Job 42:1-6 1 Job answered GOD: 2 "I'm convinced: You can do anything and everything. Nothing and no one can upset your plans. 3 You asked, 'Who is this muddying the water, ignorantly confusing the issue, second-guessing my purposes?' I admit it. I was the one. I babbled on about things far beyond me, made small talk about wonders way over my head. 4 You told me, 'Listen, and let me do the talking. Let me ask the questions. You give the answers.' 5 I admit I once lived by rumors of you; now I have it all firsthand — from my own eyes and ears! 6 I'm sorry — forgive me. I'll never do that again, I promise! I'll never again live on crusts of hearsay, crumbs of rumor."

Job finally came to a new, partial understanding of who God really is. We'll never actually come close to fully understanding a tiny part of God's enormous greatness, but it's our joy to spend the rest of our lives trying. Thank God that we don't have to rely on rumors of God; he's willing to personally reveal, the tiny part that we're capable of containing.

My Reflections and Responses:

_____

_____

_____

_____

_____

_____

Date: _____   62

Job 42:7–9 *7 After GOD had finished addressing Job, he turned to Eliphaz the Temanite and said, "I've had it with you and your two friends. I'm fed up! You haven't been honest either with me or about me — not the way my friend Job has. 8 So here's what you must do. Take seven bulls and seven rams, and go to my friend Job. Sacrifice a burnt offering on your own behalf. My friend Job will pray for you, and I will accept his prayer. He will ask me not to treat you as you deserve for talking nonsense about me, and for not being honest with me, as he has." 9 They did it. Eliphaz the Temanite, Bildad the Shuhite, and Zophar the Naamathite did what GOD commanded. And GOD accepted Job's prayer.*

God wouldn't consider forgiving Job's friends until they had made things right with Job; when they did, he did. As confused and presumptuous as Job had been to accuse God, God still called him friend and an honest man.

My Reflections and Responses:

_____

_____

_____

_____

_____

_____

_____

Date: _____   63

Job 42:10–11 *10 After Job had interceded for his friends, GOD restored his fortune — and then doubled it! 11 All his brothers and sisters and friends came to his house and celebrated. They told him how sorry they were, and consoled him for all the trouble GOD had brought him. Each of them brought generous housewarming gifts.*

In the end, his friends had to ask Job for forgiveness and he had to extend forgiveness to them for each to be restored. As wonderful as the celebration must have been, his brothers, sisters, and friends consoling Job for the trouble God had brought him, revealed that he might have learned his lesson, but they still had a thing or two to learn about God.

My Reflections and Responses:

_____

_____

_____

_____

_____

_____

_____

_____

Date: _____

Job 42:12–17 *12 GOD blessed Job's later life even more than his earlier life. He ended up with fourteen thousand sheep, six thousand camels, one thousand teams of oxen, and one thousand donkeys. 13 He also had seven sons and three daughters. 14 He named the first daughter Dove, the second, Cinnamon, and the third, Darkeyes. 15 There was not a woman in that country as beautiful as Job's daughters. Their father treated them as equals with their brothers, providing the same inheritance. 16 Job lived on another hundred and forty years, living to see his children and grandchildren — four generations of them! 17 Then he died — an old man, a full life.*

God blessed Job with more than he could have ever imagined. All that had been lost was restored many times over, and Job became an even closer friend to God, having learned more about his true nature. Having lived at the heights, fallen to the depths and been raised again, Job learned something else; he went against tradition when he provided his daughters with the same inheritance as his sons. Job learned that in the sight of God, there is no great or small, rich or poor, male or female; he loves all of his children the same and they should all be treated with the same dignity and respect.

My Reflections and Responses:

_____

_____

_____

Date: _____   65

Psalms 4:6-8 *6 Why is everyone hungry for more? "More, more," they say. "More, more." I have God's more-than-enough, 7 more joy in one ordinary day than they get in all their shopping sprees. 8 At day's end I'm ready for sound sleep, for you, GOD, have put my life back together.*

If you've ever said to yourself, "there's got to be more to life than this", you might believe in God, you might even know him, but you're not living the God life. You might be trying to fill yourself up with junk food that has no nutritional value and can never satisfy you. God's "more-than-enough" will completely fill you and conti-nually satisfy you, but he's not an appetizer, you can't have him for dessert; he has to be your whole meal or nothing at all to be your "more-than-enough".

My Reflections and Responses:

_____

_____

_____

_____

_____

_____

_____

_____

Date: _____   66

Psalms 7:9-10 *9 You get us ready for life: you probe for our soft spots, you knock off our rough edges. 10 And I'm feeling so fit, so safe: made right, kept right.*

As wonderful as it is to feel fit and safe, the process of being made right and kept right is not always a pleasant and comfortable procedure. If you think being poked where it hurts is a fun thing, you've obviously never experienced it. It you've ever knocked off the rough edges of anything, you know it's not a gentle task. Don't get confused or imagine that God isn't taking care of you just because you're going through a rough patch; he's probably paying very close attention as you're being made and kept right.

My Reflections and Responses:

_____

_____

_____

_____

_____

_____

_____

_____

Date: _____   67

Psalms 7:15-16 *15 See that man shoveling day after day, digging, then concealing, his man-trap down that lonely stretch of road? Go back and look again — you'll see him in it headfirst, legs waving in the breeze. 16 That's what happens: mischief backfires; violence boomerangs.*

Shoveling and digging day after day seems like an awful lot of work. It's amazing how much effort some people put into lying, cheating, stealing and hurting others. It appears there's a lot of hard labor involved in getting something the "easy way". If you're willing to work that hard, why not live right and make it a labor of love; you won't have to watch your back, worry about falling into your own trap, and you'll enjoy treasures on earth and in Heaven.

My Reflections and Responses:

_____

_____

_____

_____

_____

_____

_____

_____

Date: _____   68

Psalms 9:9-10 *9 GOD's a safe-house for the battered, a sanctuary during bad times. 10 The moment you arrive, you relax; you're never sorry you knocked.*

Although God hasn't exempted you from hard times or bad treatment, he is a safe-house and a sanctuary. He doesn't provide one, he is one. You don't have to go somewhere to find your sanctuary because he is always with you. A turtle carries his safe-house around on his back; you carry yours within you everywhere you go, during, not after bad times.

My Reflections and Responses:

_____

_____

_____

_____

_____

_____

_____

_____

_____

_____

Date: _____   69

Psalms 10:14 *But you know all about it — the contempt, the abuse. I dare to believe that the luckless will get lucky someday in you. You won't let them down: orphans won't be orphans forever.*

Don't think for a moment that God doesn't know all about what you're going through. Since before you were conceived he knew everything about you, all that you would go through and the plans he has for you. There is already an answer for every difficulty you face and you will always find it in him. He won't give you the solution, he is the solution. He won't tell you the answer, he is the answer. To lose yourself in him is to find yourself complete and whole with no further explanation necessary.

My Reflections and Responses:

_____

_____

_____

_____

_____

_____

_____

_____

Date: _____   70

Psalms 10:17-18 *17 The victim's faint pulse picks up; the hearts of the hopeless pump red blood as you put your ear to their lips. 18 Orphans get parents, the homeless get homes. The reign of terror is over, the rule of the gang lords is ended.*

When God shows up, everything changes. He's not just present; he puts his ear to your lips. He listens. When you join his family, you'll never be without parents or a home because he never leaves you. Your father and your lord becomes God; the balance of power has tipped and you're on the winning side forever.

My Reflections and Responses:

_____

_____

_____

_____

_____

_____

_____

_____

_____

_____

_____

Date: _____   71

Psalms 11:4 *But GOD hasn't moved to the mountains; his holy address hasn't changed. He's in charge, as always, his eyes taking everything in, his eyelids unblinking, examining Adam's unruly brood inside and out, not missing a thing.*

Have you ever lost track of someone you once knew? You lost their phone number or E-mail address and they've moved. You know they exist but have no way to get in touch of them. That will never happen with God. He never moves away, he's always the same, and his E-mail is easy to remember; God@Heaven.eternity. You can move as many times as you like but he'll never lose track of you; he never misses a thing.

My Reflections and Responses:

_____

_____

_____

_____

_____

_____

_____

_____

_____

Date: _____   72

Psalms 11:7 GOD's business is putting things right; he loves getting the lines straight, setting us straight. Once we're standing tall, we can look him straight in the eye.

Imagine how tall you'll be when God gets you all straightened out. To be able to look the creator in the eye, the very one who uses earth as his footstool; how tall must that be? It will probably take just about a lifetime to get you all untangled, totally set right and on your feet, standing tall, looking him straight in the eye for eternity; what perfect timing.

My Reflections and Responses:

_____

_____

_____

_____

_____

_____

_____

_____

_____

_____

Date: _____   73

Psalms 12:1-2 *1 Quick, GOD, I need your helping hand! The last decent person just went down, All the friends I depended on gone. 2 Everyone talks in lie language; Lies slide off their oily lips. They doubletalk with forked tongues.*

If you wait long enough, everyone on earth will let you down. Your friends will betray you, lie to you and deceive you. Before you judge them too harshly, realize this; you'll do the same to them. It's not necessarily intentional, but we're all made out of the same unreliable mud. God is the only one anyone can always count on so don't get depressed about it, just do your best and realize your own and your friends limitations.

My Reflections and Responses:

_____

_____

_____

_____

_____

_____

_____

_____

_____

Date: _____   74

Psalms 14:2-3 *2 GOD sticks his head out of heaven. He looks around. He's looking for someone not stupid — one man, even, God-expectant, just one God-ready woman. He comes up empty. A string of zeros. Useless, unshepherded sheep, taking turns pretending to be Shepherd. The ninety and nine follow their fellow.*

It's not enough to pretend you know what you're doing or where you're going; you might fool ninety nine of your fellow lost sheep but God isn't deceived. He couldn't find one man or woman ready for him so he sent Jesus. We finally have a real leader who not only knows the way but is the Way the Truth and the Life.

My Reflections and Responses:

_____

_____

_____

_____

_____

_____

_____

_____

_____

Date: _____

Psalms 15 GOD, who gets invited to dinner at your place? How do we get on your guest list? 2 "Walk straight, act right, tell the truth. 3 "Don't hurt your friend, don't blame your neighbor; 4 despise the despicable."Keep your word even when it costs you, 5 make an honest living, never take a bribe. "You'll never get blacklisted if you live like this."

I t seems pretty straight forward; if you want to get invited to dinner at God's place, do those simple things you've just read and you'll be on the permanent guest list. The problem is, no one, on their own, has ever been able to do those few simple things. The solution is to join God's family. All meals at his house are family affairs; as a member of the family, all those things you could never do on your own have already been done for you by another member of the family, Jesus. You'll be dining with the King's trio, Father, Son and Holy Spirit from now on.

My Reflections and Responses:

_____

_____

_____

_____

_____

_____

Date: _____   76

Psalms 16:11 *Now you've got my feet on the life path, all radiant from the shining of your face. Ever since you took my hand, I'm on the right way.*

You can't walk the life path alone, no matter how sincere you are or how hard you try. One step without faith is a step in the wrong direction. When, with your permission, God takes your hand in his, and Jesus is God's hand, you'll be on the right way because he is the way. Any other way has got to be the wrong way.

My Reflections and Responses:

_____

_____

_____

_____

_____

_____

_____

_____

_____

_____

_____

Date: _____   77

Psalms 17:3 *Go ahead, examine me from inside out, surprise me in the middle of the night — You'll find I'm just what I say I am. My words don't run loose.*

When David invited God to check him out, he wasn't bragging and he wasn't saying that God would find a perfect man, just a genuine one. David needed to rely on God's grace and forgiveness many times throughout his life because he was far from perfect. He was a man after God's own heart because he never stopped chasing after God's heart, not because he was without flaws. Are you ready to stand up to such a surprise inspection in the middle of the night, when you least expect it? If not, why not? If not now, when?

My Reflections and Responses:

_____

_____

_____

_____

_____

_____

_____

_____

Date: _____   78

Psalms 17:4-5 *4 I'm not trying to get my way in the world's way. I'm trying to get your way, your Word's way. 5 I'm staying on your trail; I'm putting one foot in front of the other. I'm not giving up.*

Don't try to live your own life your own way; you'll miss out on your real life with Him forever. Don't even try to live a Godly life; it's way too much to even attempt. Just make your next step a God step, then another and another; with his help, you'll get there one step at a time.

My Reflections and Responses:

_____

_____

_____

_____

_____

_____

_____

_____

_____

_____

_____

Date: _____   79

Psalms 18:6 *A hostile world! I call to GOD, I cry to God to help me. From his palace he hears my call; my cry brings me right into his presence — a private audience!*

If you're in need of a private moment with God, in a hurry, while you're doing your best to hold off a hostile world, just cry out to him; he'll hear you and be there instantly. When you call on the Lord you don't have to wait; you go to the head of the line and get his attention immediately. He was actually there all along but your cry will make you aware of his presence and it will be of great comfort and tremendous strength.

My Reflections and Responses:

_____

_____

_____

_____

_____

_____

_____

_____

_____

_____

Date: _____   80

Psalms 18:16-19 *16 But me he caught — reached all the way from sky to sea; he pulled me out of that ocean of hate, 17 that enemy chaos, the void in which I was drowning. 18 They hit me when I was down, but GOD stuck by me. 19 He stood me up on a wide-open field; I stood there*

What a surprise and how indescribably wonderful; there is no distance that you can travel, no situation that you can get yourself into and no hideous act that you can commit that can ever separate you from your father's love. His love for you is not dependent on your worthiness but on his wonderfulness. Thank God, thank him again.

My Reflections and Responses:

_____

_____

_____

_____

_____

_____

_____

_____

_____

Date: _____

Psalms 18:20-24 *20 GOD made my life complete when I placed all the pieces before him. When I got my act together, he gave me a fresh start. 21 Now I'm alert to GOD's ways; I don't take God for granted. 22 Every day I review the ways he works; I try not to miss a trick. 23 I feel put back together, and I'm watching my step. 24 GOD rewrote the text of my life when I opened the book of my heart to his eyes.*

You can't put all the pieces of your life back together and you can't rewrite the text of your life; only God can do that. What you can do, and must do, if you want God to do what only he can do, is place the broken pieces of your life before him and open your heart to him so he can and will do the rest. After he's transformed you, pay close attention to his ways and do your best to walk in his footprints; otherwise you'll begin to fall to pieces again. He'll put you back together again but why make extra work for him.

My Reflections and Responses:

_____

_____

_____

_____

_____

_____

Date: _____   82

Psalms 18:28-30 *28 Suddenly, GOD, you floodlight my life; I'm blazing with glory, God's glory! 29 I smash the bands of marauders, I vault the highest fences. 30 What a God! His road stretches straight and smooth. Every GOD-direction is road-tested. Everyone who runs toward him makes it.*

What a wonderful description of being filled and empowered by the Holy Spirit many generations before Jesus sent his Spirit to live inside of us permanently. When you're filled and walking in the Spirit, every road is a God road. If you run to him, he promises you'll make it; anything less than an all out, totally committed run comes with no such guarantee.

My Reflections and Responses:

_____

_____

_____

_____

_____

_____

_____

_____

_____

Date: _____   83

Psalms 19:7-8 *7 The revelation of GOD is whole and pulls our lives together. The signposts of GOD are clear and point out the right road. 8 The life-maps of GOD are right, showing the way to joy. The directions of GOD are plain and easy on the eyes.*

Whether its revelation, signposts, life-maps or directions, God's desire is that we find our way to him so he goes out of his way to make it as easy as possible. His Word is complete, concise and includes absolutely everything we need, to know him, which starts with simply knowing about him, then wanting to know him personally and finally desiring to serve and give ourselves completely to him.

My Reflections and Responses:

_____

_____

_____

_____

_____

_____

_____

_____

Date: _____   84

Psalms 19:11-13 *11 There's more: God's Word warns us of danger and directs us to hidden treasure. 12 Otherwise how will we find our way? Or know when we play the fool? 13 Clean the slate, God, so we can start the day fresh! Keep me from stupid sins, from thinking I can take over your work; Then I can start this day sun-washed, scrubbed clean of the grime of sin.*

If you want a description of stupid, what's more stupid than thinking we can do God's job. His Word tells us what our job is, keeps us safe, and as a bonus, is a treasure map to hidden marvels. If you want to start each day sun and Son-washed, expect to need a good scrubbing by the end of the day, every day.

My Reflections and Responses:

_____

_____

_____

_____

_____

_____

_____

_____

_____

Date: _____

Psalms 22:6-8 *6 And here I am, a nothing — an earthworm, something to step on, to squash. 7 Everyone pokes fun at me; they make faces at me, they shake their heads: 8 "Let's see how GOD handles this one; since God likes him so much, let him help him!"*

You might at times act like an earthworm and on a bad hair day even look like one, but don't let anyone convince you that you are one. Go ahead and let them see how God handles you; with all the love, care, tenderness and dignity he reserves for one of his favorites, because you are. They might learn a thing or two and their heads might just start shaking the other direction.

My Reflections and Responses:

_____

_____

_____

_____

_____

_____

_____

_____

_____

Date: _____   86

Psalms 22:27-28 *27 From the four corners of the earth people are coming to their senses, are running back to GOD. Long-lost families are falling on their faces before him. 28 GOD has taken charge; from now on he has the last word.*

When the world is at its worst, governments have failed us, religion has failed us and we have failed ourselves, what's left but to turn to the one who made us. Think of the trouble we could have avoided if we'd turned to him first, but it never seems to happen that way. Thank God for his mercy and grace and patience with a stubborn people. He had the first word, he spoke the world into existence; he will have the last word, calling an end to this age; maybe we should be in his Word in the meantime.

My Reflections and Responses:

_____

_____

_____

_____

_____

_____

_____

_____

Date: _____

Psalms 22:30-31 *30 Our children and their children will get in on this as the word is passed along from parent to child. 31 Babies not yet conceived will hear the good news — that God does what he says.*

How will our children and their children get in on the good news of we don't pass it on to them? Would you let your children miss out on what other children enjoy just because you didn't pass it on? Because God always does what he says, it doesn't matter when he says it, it will always be true. You don't have to check out its authenticity before you pass it on, and God doesn't have to keep repeating himself once he's told you something.

My Reflections and Responses:

_____

_____

_____

_____

_____

_____

_____

_____

Date: _____

Psalms 26:2-3 *2 Examine me, GOD, from head to foot, order your battery of tests. Make sure I'm fit inside and out 3 So I never lose sight of your love, but keep in step with you, never missing a beat.*

If you ever feel unloved by God, you can be sure the connection has been broken on your end, not his. His love doesn't come and go, stop and start; it only comes and comes and comes. David wasn't afraid that God would stop loving him, only that he might lose sight of that love. He was willing to undergo the most stringent internal and external examination to insure that never happened. First, do your own examination and take care of what you can, then invite God to completely check you out, fix you up and set you on the right path; it's the only way you can "keep in step and never miss a beat".

My Reflections and Responses:

_____

_____

_____

_____

_____

_____

_____

Date: _____   89

Psalms 27:1-3 *1 Light, space, zest — that's GOD! So, with him on my side I'm fearless, afraid of no one and nothing. 2 When vandal hordes ride down ready to eat me alive, those bullies and toughs fall flat on their faces. 3 When besieged, I'm calm as a baby. When all hell breaks loose, I'm collected and cool.*

God illuminates your path and your life; he is light. God doesn't suffocate or micromanage you; he is space. God passes on his enthusiasm for life to you; he is zest. You can remain calm, cool and collected, whatever the situation, because he is your solution in every situation.

My Reflections and Responses:

_____

_____

_____

_____

_____

_____

_____

_____

_____

_____

Date: _____   90

Psalms 27:4-5 *4 I'm asking GOD for one thing, only one thing: To live with him in his house my whole life long. I'll contemplate his beauty; I'll study at his feet. 5 That's the only quiet, secure place in a noisy world, the perfect getaway, far from the buzz of traffic.*

David wasn't talking about spending eternity in heaven with God; he was talking about living with him in his house right here on earth. Don't think you have to wait till you get to heaven to start living with God in his house. His house isn't a building or location; it's anywhere he abides. If you abide in him and he in you, take off your coat, kick of your shoes, you're home.

My Reflections and Responses:

_____

_____

_____

_____

_____

_____

_____

_____

_____

Date: _____

Psalms 31:9-10 *9 Be kind to me, GOD — I'm in deep, deep trouble again. I've cried my eyes out; I feel hollow inside. 10 My life leaks away, groan by groan; my years fade out in sighs. My troubles have worn me out, turned my bones to powder.*

Without God's lifeblood, his DNA, we're in deep trouble and begin to age quickly. To truly remain alive, we're in desperate need of a transfusion. We've already been typed and matched; the only blood we can use is the blood of Jesus. Because he hadn't yet shed his blood and sent his Holy Spirit to stay with us permanently, David kept ending up empty, in need of a refill. Since Jesus came, things are different. We never have to run dry and end up empty again.

My Reflections and Responses:

_____

_____

_____

_____

_____

_____

_____

Date: _____

Psalms 33:1-3 *1 Good people, cheer GOD! Right-living people sound best when praising. 2 Use guitars to reinforce your Hallelujahs! Play his praise on a grand piano! 3 Invent your own new song to him; give him a trumpet fanfare.*

Your best sound is the one you make when you praise God; it's what your vocal cords were made for. God gave you a voice and a choice. He will be praised and you can choose to be the one who does it; if you won't, the rocks will. Why let the rocks have all the fun. Explore and invent new ways to praise him. Everything you do as a Hallelujah to him will be glorious music to his ears. Take a chance; you can't go wrong if your heart's right.

My Reflections and Responses:

_____

_____

_____

_____

_____

_____

_____

_____

Date: _____

Psalms 34:8-9 *8 Open your mouth and taste, open your eyes and see — how good GOD is. Blessed are you who run to him. 9 Worship GOD if you want the best; worship opens doors to all his goodness.*

If you listen closely, you will hear God speak to you in many different ways but did you know that you can actually taste and see how good he is. Let every one of your senses experience and enjoy God. Become so attuned to his presence that you don't have to rely only on feeling him to know he's there. God's goodness is so enormous, you'll never run out of doors to open, discovering an endless supply of goodness; worship is the key that unlocks every one.

My Reflections and Responses:

_____

_____

_____

_____

_____

_____

_____

_____

Date: _____   94

Psalms 34:17-19 *17 Is anyone crying for help? GOD is listening, ready to rescue you. 18 If your heart is broken, you'll find GOD right there; if you're kicked in the gut, he'll help you catch your breath. 19 Disciples so often get into trouble; still, GOD is there every time.*

God cares about everything so he gets involved in everything and as his disciple, you'll be right there with him. With all that involvement in humanity, you're bound to get into trouble frequently. Sometimes it will be the fault of others who don't like God or you meddling in their affairs; sometimes you'll cause the trouble yourself out of disobedience, misunderstanding or over enthusiasm. It doesn't matter whose fault it is, God will be there every time to keep getting you out of trouble. He especially loves to mend your broken heart because getting your heart broken means you let your heart get involved; he's all about that.

My Reflections and Responses:

_____

_____

_____

_____

_____

_____

Date: _____   95

Psalms 35:9-10 *9 But let me run loose and free, celebrating GOD's great work, 10 Every bone in my body laughing, singing, "GOD, there's no one like you. You put the down-and-out on their feet and protect the unprotected from bullies!"*

If God puts the down-and-out on their feet and protects the unprotected, what do you have to worry about? If you're not running loose and free, why not? If anything is ever going to inspire you to laugh and sing, let it be God. There's work to be done, sadness to be experienced and tragedy to get through during your time here on earth, but remember, you're a child of God; don't forget to spend much of your time enjoying and celebrating that incredible reality.

My Reflections and Responses:

_____

_____

_____

_____

_____

_____

_____

_____

Date: _____   96

Psalms 36:5-6 *5 God's love is meteoric, his loyalty astronomic, 6 His purpose titanic, his verdicts oceanic. Yet in his largeness nothing gets lost; not a man, not a mouse, slips through the cracks.*

When describing God, there's no such thing as hyperbole. You simply can't exaggerate or overstate his magnificence. Incredibly, his largeness doesn't diminish your existence; his presence magnifies your importance because he shares his greatness with you.

My Reflections and Responses:

_____

_____

_____

_____

_____

_____

_____

_____

_____

_____

_____

_____

Date: _____

Psalms 37:5-7 *5 Open up before GOD, keep nothing back; he'll do whatever needs to be done: 6 He'll validate your life in the clear light of day and stamp you with approval at high noon. 7 Quiet down before GOD, be prayerful before him. Don't bother with those who climb the ladder, who elbow their way to the top.*

Open up to God so he can do whatever needs to be done; if you don't, he can't. It's not that he lacks the ability; he's God and can do anything, but keeping something from him, as if he doesn't know anyway, is like telling him you don't want his help. He gave you a free will, and if you refuse his help, he won't force it on you. When you're in God's presence, you can relax and calm down. You don't need to get caught up in the race with those who push, shove and step all over each other just to get ahead; when you're in his presence, you're already right where you want to be.

My Reflections and Responses:

_____

_____

_____

_____

_____

_____

Date: _____   98

Psalms 37:12-15 *12 Bad guys have it in for the good guys, obsessed with doing them in. 13 But GOD isn't losing any sleep; to him they're a joke with no punch line. 14 Bullies brandish their swords, pull back on their bows with a flourish. They're out to beat up on the harmless, or mug that nice man out walking his dog. 15 A banana peel lands them flat on their faces — slapstick figures in a moral circus.*

There will always be bad guys going around looking for an opportunity to pick on the good guys. You're one of the good guys and if God isn't losing any sleep over them, why should you. Avoid them if possible, no one enjoys putting up with that kind of aggravation, but don't be afraid and don't spend too much time think about them; you've got much better things to think about, and sooner or later they'll find out what happens when you pick on God's kids.

My Reflections and Responses:

_____

_____

_____

_____

_____

_____

_____

Date: _____

Psalms 37:16-19 *16 Less is more and more is less. One righteous will outclass fifty wicked, 17 for the wicked are moral weaklings but the righteous are GOD-strong. 18 GOD keeps track of the decent folk; what they do won't soon be forgotten. 19 In hard times, they'll hold their heads high; when the shelves are bare, they'll be full.*

There is a great reversal going on among God's people and his Word refers to it many times. Less is more, weak is strong, lose your life to find it. God wisdom is not conventional wisdom and his plans are not man's plans. Being God-strong involves qualities the world would call weak; love, patience, humility, sacrifice, tenderness, gentleness. Don't be surprised if he asks you for more faith and less effort; it's just part of his great reversal. Don't try too hard to figure it out; just enjoy the confused looks you get from the world when you consistently accomplish more with less; it becomes a testimony of God's greatness, not yours.

My Reflections and Responses:

_____

_____

_____

_____

_____

_____

Date: _____   100

Psalms 38:17-22 *17 I'm on the edge of losing it — the pain in my gut keeps burning. 18 I'm ready to tell my story of failure, I'm no longer smug in my sin. 19 My enemies are alive and in action, a lynch mob after my neck. 20 I give out good and get back evil from God-haters who can't stand a God-lover. 21 Don't dump me, GOD; my God, don't stand me up. 22 Hurry and help me; I want some wide-open space in my life!*

Being a God-lover who goes around doing good deeds isn't enough. A man after God's on heart was on the edge of disaster, ready to concede. He was no match for his enemies who were about to string him up. His arrogance and self-indulgence caused him to lose sight of where his real strength came from and the world was closing in on him. Loving God and doing good is good, but not sufficient; obeying him, relying on him, and taking his path, not your own, are also essential ingredients in your successful walk with him.

My Reflections and Responses:

_____

_____

_____

_____

_____

_____

Date: _____   101

Psalms 40:1-3 *1 I waited and waited and waited for GOD. At last he looked; finally he listened. 2 He lifted me out of the ditch, pulled me from deep mud. He stood me up on a solid rock to make sure I wouldn't slip. 3 He taught me how to sing the latest God-song, a praise-song to our God. More and more people are seeing this: they enter the mystery, abandoning themselves to GOD.*

Waiting and waiting and waiting sounds just a little bit impatient. Do you really think God doesn't see everything? Is it possible that he is sometimes distracted and doesn't hear or even care about the smallest detail of your life? No, that's not possible; he has promised that nothing escapes his attention, but his timing is perfect, ours isn't. Wait on him but don't wait and wait and wait, tapping your feet, looking at the clock or calendar. Look what happens when the time is right; he lifts you up, sets you on solid rock, and teaches you a new God-song. Join all the others who are losing themselves in God and you won't be keeping track of time.

My Reflections and Responses:

_____

_____

_____

_____

Psalms 40:4-5 *4 Blessed are you who give yourselves over to GOD, turn your backs on the world's "sure thing," ignore what the world worships; 5 The world's a huge stockpile of GOD-wonders and God-thoughts. Nothing and no one comes close to you! I start talking about you, telling what I know, and quickly run out of words. Neither numbers nor words account for you.*

Have you ever tried to go two ways at once? You end up stuck, going nowhere. Giving yourself over to God and turning your back on the world is one act, not two. If you really do the first, the other automatically happens. If you get caught up in the worlds "sure thing", you haven't given yourself over to God quit yet; when you do, you'll discover that what you experience can't be adequately described, categorized or even fully comprehended. Because of this phenomenon, you can't ever really know it until you do it so just jump in; it's called a leap of faith.

My Reflections and Responses:

_____

_____

_____

_____

_____

_____

Date: _____

Psalms 40:6-8 *6 Doing something for you, bringing something to you — that's not what you're after. Being religious, acting pious — that's not what you're asking for. You've opened my ears so I can listen. 7 So I answered, "I'm coming. I read in your letter what you wrote about me, 8 and I'm coming to the party you're throwing for me." That's when God's Word entered my life, became part of my very being.*

If you spend your life doing things for God, earning things from him, and being as religious as you possibly can, you'll end up exhausted but never really pleasing him. He's the creator and owner of everything; what could you possibly give him that he doesn't already have? There is one thing that he doesn't have without your cooperation, you. When he created you, he gave you a free will, limiting his ability to have the one thing he really wants from you without your participation; a relationship with you, the one he loves. When you understand that it's all about his love for you, his Word has finally become a part of your very being.

My Reflections and Responses:

_____

_____

_____

_____

_____

Date: _____   104

Psalms 40:16-17 *16 Let those who know what you're all about tell the world you're great and not quitting. 17 And me? I'm a mess. I'm nothing and have nothing: make something of me. You can do it; you've got what it takes — but God, don't put it off.*

It's all right to be a mess, God can work with that; just admit it and let him go to work straightening things out. Those who go around pretending they have it all together are the ones in real trouble. When you realize you are nothing and have nothing without God, you're exactly where he needs you to be so he can make you into what you were always intended to be, something wonderful, and give you what he's always wanted you to have, everything, including eternal life with him. You won't have to wait; he's the one who has been waiting for you.

My Reflections and Responses:

_____

_____

_____

_____

_____

_____

_____

Date: _____

Psalms 42:5 *Why are you down in the dumps, dear soul? Why are you crying the blues? Fix my eyes on God — soon I'll be praising again. He puts a smile on my face. He's my God.*

If you're discouraged and depressed, your soul might need to be reminded that you are a child of God; it's alright to talk to yourself and be your own encourager. When your eyes are on God, they're not on you and things will start looking much better. It's when we turn inward, becoming self-focused, that we begin to magnify and amplify all of the negatives. Put anything under a powerful enough microscope and it begins to look like a monster.

My Reflections and Responses:

_____

_____

_____

_____

_____

_____

_____

_____

_____

Psalms 42:6-8 *6 When my soul is in the dumps, I rehearse everything I know of you, from Jordan depths to Hermon heights, including Mount Mizar. 7 Chaos calls to chaos, to the tune of whitewater rapids. Your breaking surf, your thundering breakers crash and crush me. 8 Then GOD promises to love me all day, sing songs all through the night! My life is God's prayer.*

Medical science has made us aware of neurological, physiological, biochemical and genetic reasons for depression. Antidepressants have been developed to address those aspects of depression that are beyond our ability to correct with a positive attitude and a grateful heart. Medicine isn't man made; its God made, man discovered and one of his many ways of providing for his children when appropriately used. Don't hesitate to take necessary medication; it's a gift from God, but it will never replace your responsibility to live right, think right and be the right person. If you're depressed, remind yourself of the blessings and security that come with being in his presence, not the chaos and destruction that's sure to crush you the moment you decide to go it alone. You and your decisions will always play a crucial role in your own wellbeing; there's no adequate substitution.

My Reflections and Responses:

_____

Date: _____   107

Psalms 43:3-4 *3 Give me your lantern and compass, give me a map, so I can find my way to the sacred mountain, to the place of your presence, 4 to enter the place of worship, meet my exuberant God, sing my thanks with a harp, magnificent God, my God.*

Jesus promised if you look for him, you will find him; not because on your own you will ever discover the way to God, but because he has already found you. Jesus is your lantern, compass and map to God. When you get there, you will know exactly what to do. Everyone who comes into the presence of God knows what to do, because there's nothing else to do; worship him, magnify him and sing praises to him. You won't need to ask him for anything because being with him is everything.

My Reflections and Responses:

_____

_____

_____

_____

_____

_____

_____

Psalms 44:23-26 *23 Get up, GOD! Are you going to sleep all day? Wake up! Don't you care what happens to us? 24 Why do you bury your face in the pillow? Why pretend things are just fine with us? 25 And here we are — flat on our faces in the dirt, held down with a boot on our necks. 26 Get up and come to our rescue. If you love us so much, Help us!*

Isn't it amazing how, the moment we lose sight of God, we assume he's lost sight of us? We fall asleep on the job, wake up, and immediately conclude that he's the one who's been sleeping. While it might be anatomically impossible, it's often our own boot on our neck that rubs our face in the dirt. Get up, look up, and discover that he's been there all along; waiting patiently to lift you up out of the mess you've gotten yourself into.

My Reflections and Responses:

_____

_____

_____

_____

_____

_____

_____

_____

Date: _____   109

Psalms 49:10-15 *10 Anyone can see that the brightest and best die, wiped out right along with fools and dunces. 11 They leave all their prowess behind, move into their new home, the coffin, the cemetery their permanent address. And to think they named counties after themselves! 12 We aren't immortal. We don't last long. Like our dogs, we age and weaken. And die. 13 This is what happens to those who live for the moment, who only look out for themselves: 14 Death herds them like sheep straight to hell; they disappear down the gullet of the grave; they waste away to nothing — nothing left but a marker in a cemetery. 15 But me? God snatches me from the clutch of death, he reaches down and grabs me.*

If we live only for the moment, for our petty self-indulgences, our tombstone will mark the end to the best we can ever hope to experience in this life or the next. If we choose to live a life no different than our dogs, they will have lived a far better life than us. At least they didn't have to make a living, worry about paying taxes or concern themselves with obeying the law. If we live to love God and others, we will have lived a large and satisfying life here on earth, having enjoyed and contributed to the best this world has to offer, and death will not be the end, just the end of the beginning and the beginning of eternity with him.

My Reflections and Responses:

_____

_____

Date: _____

Psalms 51:1-3 *1 Generous in love — God, give grace! Huge in mercy — wipe out my bad record. 2 Scrub away my guilt, soak out my sins in your laundry. 3 I know how bad I've been; my sins are staring me down.*

To fully appreciate how good God is, we need to understand how bad we really are. Take a complete inventory of all the awful, disgusting, inexcusable things you've ever participated in. Now rip your list into little pieces, burn it up and get rid of the ashes because you never have to remember it again; God doesn't. When you accepted Jesus as your Lord and Savior, your past, present and future lists were all taken care of ; that's how good, wonderful, generous and forgiving God is. If you haven't accepted Jesus yet, that's what you can look forward to as soon as you do.

My Reflections and Responses:

_____

_____

_____

_____

_____

_____

_____

Date: _____

Psalms 51:7-15 *7 Soak me in your laundry and I'll come out clean, scrub me and I'll have a snow-white life. 8 Tune me in to foot-tapping songs, set these once-broken bones to dancing. 9 Don't look too close for blemishes, give me a clean bill of health. 10 God, make a fresh start in me, shape a Genesis week from the chaos of my life. 11 Don't throw me out with the trash, or fail to breathe holiness in me. 12 Bring me back from gray exile, put a fresh wind in my sails! 13 Give me a job teaching rebels your ways so the lost can find their way home. 14 Commute my death sentence, God, my salvation God, and I'll sing anthems to your life-giving ways. 15 Unbutton my lips, dear God; I'll let loose with your praise.*

In a moment of extreme clarity, David realized and expressed his total dependence on God for everything. No aspect of your life will ever come into full alignment without complete unity with him, which can only be accomplished through a relationship with his son Jesus. You were not created to be independent or self-sufficient; without him you will always feel like a part of you is missing, because it is. When you finally become filled and fulfilled with God, you'll want to sing and shout praises to him but you won't even be able to do that until he "unbuttons" your lips.

My Reflections and Responses:

_____

_____

_____

Date: _____

Psalms 51:16-17 *16 Going through the motions doesn't please you, a flawless performance is nothing to you. 17 I learned God-worship when my pride was shattered. Heart-shattered lives ready for love don't for a moment escape God's notice.*

P ride is like an invisible shield that keeps everything and everyone from penetrating; until it's shattered, there's no chance of ever reaching your most vital organ, your heart; the place where love lives. If you really want to love and be loved, you're heart's the next thing that needs to be broken. As long as it remains intact, hardened to the possibility of pain or vulnerability, you're still not quite ready for love. When love becomes so important that your pride is destroyed and your heart is breaking and aching for it, you'll gladly drop all of your defenses and God will know, you're ready for love.

My Reflections and Responses:

_____

_____

_____

_____

_____

_____

Date: _____   113

Psalms 56:1-4 *1 Take my side, God — I'm getting kicked around, stomped on every day. 2 Not a day goes by but somebody beats me up; they make it their duty to beat me up. 3 When I get really afraid I come to you in trust. 4 I'm proud to praise God; fearless now, I trust in God. What can mere mortals do?*

Don't wait until you're really afraid before you go to God. By then you've already put up with far more than he intended. Go to him for everything, big or small, so often that you don't have to ask him to take your side; you'll stay by his side. If you do find yourself afraid, start praising God; it will embolden you and remind you of whose child you are. How can you stay afraid and trust God at the same time?

My Reflections and Responses:

_____

_____

_____

_____

_____

_____

_____

_____

Date: _____   114

Psalms 62:1-2 *1 God, the one and only — I'll wait as long as he says. Everything I need comes from him, so why not? 2 He's solid rock under my feet, breathing room for my soul, An impregnable castle: I'm set for life.*

God's timing is perfect and not subject to change because of your impatience. You might as well settle down and get comfortable with it because he has all the time in the world and he's taking it. He won't be hurried but he won't rush you either. You'll have everything you need when you need it so relax and enjoy the peace and security that comes with realizing that he is extravagantly generous and you are one of his favorites.

My Reflections and Responses:

Date: _____

Psalms 66:16-20 *16 All believers, come here and listen, let me tell you what God did for me. 17 I called out to him with my mouth, my tongue shaped the sounds of music. 18 If I had been cozy with evil, the Lord would never have listened. 19 But he most surely did listen, he came on the double when he heard my prayer. 20 Blessed be God: he didn't turn a deaf ear, he stayed with me, loyal in his love.*

When God blesses you, don't keep it quiet. Tell everyone you know what a good God he is and how he listens to you. When you're in need, who are you going to call out to, someone close to you or someone far away? If you're comfortable with evil, that's where you'll first turn for help before you even think about calling to the Lord; you might be wasting precious time. If you're comfortable and cozy with the Lord, calling on him will be the most natural thing in the world to do, and he's always listening for the sound of his children.

My Reflections and Responses:

_____

_____

_____

_____

_____

_____

Date: _____   116

Psalms 71:1-3 1 I run for dear life to GOD, I'll never live to regret it. 2 Do what you do so well: get me out of this mess and up on my feet. Put your ear to the ground and listen, give me space for salvation. 3 Be a guest room where I can retreat; you said your door was always open! You're my salvation — my vast, granite fortress.

When do you run for dear life; when your dear life is in big trouble and you'd like to save it? When does your dear life get into that kind of mess? Trouble of that magnitude usually happens when someone isn't listening to the Lord; it might be your enemy or it might even be you. God is always listening and his door is always open so remember where your safety lies and don't be slow to go there; you'll never regret it. You're free to go in and out of an open door, but here's a thought; why not make that guest room your permanent living room?

My Reflections and Responses:

_____

_____

_____

_____

_____

_____

Date: _____   117

Psalms 73:1-5 *1 No doubt about it! God is good — good to good people, good to the good-hearted. 2 But I nearly missed it, missed seeing his goodness. 3 I was looking the other way, looking up to the people 4 at the top, envying the wicked who have it made, 5 who have nothing to worry about, not a care in the whole wide world.*

Don't look to the people who appear to be successful by worldly standards; the ones who seem to have everything anyone could ever want. They have nothing to worry about because they don't bother worrying over the likes of you. It's God who looks after you and all the other ordinary folks who need looking after. The ones who think they need no help, from God, you or anyone else have nothing to teach you. One day they will discover that self-help is no help at all and anything that doesn't come from God isn't worth having and won't last anyway. Because you looked in the right direction, you see his goodness and experience his grace.

My Reflections and Responses:

_____

_____

_____

_____

_____

Date: _____   118

Psalms 73:25-28 25 You're all I want in heaven! You're all I want on earth! 26 When my skin sags and my bones get brittle, GOD is rock-firm and faithful. 27 Look! Those who left you are falling apart! Deserters, they'll never be heard from again. 28 But I'm in the very presence of God — oh, how refreshing it is! I've made Lord GOD my home. God, I'm telling the world what you do!

God willing, you will live a long time and near the end of that time your body, your bones, your eyesight and probably even your heart will begin to fail you. If you've made Lord God your home here on earth, you truly have a mobile home that will go with you wherever you go, even heaven. Your body isn't really your home, meant to last forever; it's just a temporary shelter provided by God to contain yours and his spirits during your short time here on earth. What we call old age and eventually death, is that time in your life when your body has served its purpose and is releasing your spirit, which was created to last forever; freeing it from the temporal to its immortal, eternal destiny with your Lord. Your home won't change, he's always with you; just your view.

My Reflections and Responses:

_____

_____

_____

Date: _____   119

Psalms 100 *On your feet now — applaud GOD! 2 Bring a gift of laughter, sing yourselves into his presence. 3 Know this: GOD is God, and God, GOD. He made us; we didn't make him. We're his people, his well-tended sheep. 4 Enter with the password: "Thank you!" Make yourselves at home, talking praise. Thank him. Worship him. 5 For GOD is sheer beauty, all-generous in love, loyal always and ever.*

If you want to live in God's presence always then praise him continuously. He inhabits your worship and praise. If you feel distant from him, sing yourself into an awareness of his presence. If you get so caught up in praise to him that you forget to ask for anything, don't worry; he knows what you need before you ask, and is an extremely generous father. You won't miss out on a thing. Thank him for what he's done for you, for what he's doing for you, for what he's going to do for you, but most of all, thank him for being GOD, which is just another way of thanking him for everything.

My Reflections and Responses:

_____

_____

_____

_____

_____

Date: _____   120

Psalms 102:18-22 *18 Write this down for the next generation so people not yet born will praise GOD: 19 "GOD looked out from his high holy place; from heaven he surveyed the earth. 20 He listened to the groans of the doomed, he opened the doors of their death cells." 21 Write it so the story can be told in Zion, so GOD's praise will be sung in Jerusalem's streets 22 and wherever people gather together along with their rulers to worship him.*

It's important to tell your own personal story of what it means to have God in your life, but don't forget to write it down for future generations. God reveals and makes himself famous to each generation, but they won't know to praise him for all the wonderful things he's been doing since the beginning of time unless those from the past remember to write their own stories down. Where would we be if the Bible had never been written down?

My Reflections and Responses:

_____

_____

_____

_____

_____

_____

Date: _____

Psalms 104:24-30 *24 What a wildly wonderful world, GOD! You made it all, with Wisdom at your side, made earth overflow with your wonderful creations. 25 Oh, look — the deep, wide sea, brimming with fish past counting, sardines and sharks and salmon. 26 Ships plow those waters, and Leviathan, your pet dragon, romps in them. 27 All the creatures look expectantly to you to give them their meals on time. 28 You come, and they gather around; you open your hand and they eat from it. 29 If you turned your back, they'd die in a minute — Take back your Spirit and they die, revert to original mud; 30 Send out your Spirit and they spring to life — the whole countryside in bloom and blossom.*

God placed inside each of us the ability and desire to recognize and enjoy beauty and replicate it whenever and wherever we can. Stores, museums, and theaters are full of our best attempts at recreating the beauty found in nature, God's art gallery. In all our creative attempts at making something beautiful, there's something lacking. Our most prized collections are missing the one ingredient that only God's artwork contains; life. Without his spirit, the earth, everything on it and everyone in it becomes mud. Enjoy the "wildly wonderful world" his spirit created; thank him for it, and try your hand at copying it, but remember it's just a copy; there's only one original.

My Reflections and Responses:

_____

_____

Date: _____   122

Psalms 105:1-5 *1 Thank GOD! Pray to him by name! Tell everyone you meet what he has done! 2 Sing him songs, belt out hymns, translate his wonders into music! 3 Honor his holy name with Hallelujahs, you who seek GOD. Live a happy life! 4 Keep your eyes open for GOD, watch for his works; be alert for signs of his presence. 5 Remember the world of wonders he has made, his miracles, and the verdicts he's rendered —*

If you're paying attention, it will be impossible to forget God; the signs of his presence, including his wonders, works and miracles, are everywhere. If you're looking for him, worship and praise him with Hallelujahs and you'll begin to sense his presence immediately. Don't pray for a happy life; live a happy life. If you know God, you have the entire ingredients necessary for that happy life you're looking for; go ahead and live it.

My Reflections and Responses:

_____

_____

_____

_____

_____

_____

_____

Date: _____

Psalms 107:4-8 *4 Some of you wandered for years in the desert, looking but not finding a good place to live, 5 Half-starved and parched with thirst, staggering and stumbling, on the brink of exhaustion. 6 Then, in your desperate condition, you called out to GOD. He got you out in the nick of time; 7 He put your feet on a wonderful road that took you straight to a good place to live. 8 So thank GOD for his marvelous love, for his miracle mercy to the children he loves.*

What you've been looking for all your life and never finding on your own, God can give you in a moment. His first and greatest gift is eternal salvation through his son Jesus; that alone would make a life lived for him worth everything, but he's extravagantly generous with his children. When you call out to God, you get your needs met, your dreams fulfilled, your heart mended and in his presence, you never grow old. Your body will wear out, but the real you will be young forever; the original fountain of youth.

My Reflections and Responses:

_____

_____

_____

_____

_____

_____

Date: _____

Psalms 107:17-21 *17 Some of you were sick because you'd lived a bad life, your bodies feeling the effects of your sin; 18 You couldn't stand the sight of food, so miserable you thought you'd be better off dead. 19 Then you called out to GOD in your desperate condition; he got you out in the nick of time. 20 He spoke the word that healed you, that pulled you back from the brink of death. 21 So thank GOD for his marvelous love, for his miracle mercy to the children he loves...*

S ometimes we get sick because we get to close to someone with a contagious disease. Sometimes we inherit weakness that predisposes us to illness. Sometimes accidents weaken our bodies and we succumb to infection. Sometimes we just get old and our immune systems finally ware out. Some of us have lived bad lives and our sins have begun to destroy our bodies, minds and spirits. Whatever caused our desperate condition, God is the answer to our dilemma. Call out to him and he will rescue you even if it takes a mercy miracle.

My Reflections and Responses:

_____

_____

_____

_____

_____

Date: _____

Psalms 119:1-3 *1 You're blessed when you stay on course, walking steadily on the road revealed by GOD. 2 You're blessed when you follow his directions, doing your best to find him. 3 That's right — you don't go off on your own; you walk straight along the road he set.*

God loves you whether you always stay on course or not. He will forgive you and set you back on the right road as many times as you ask. Being blessed is not the same as being loved or forgiven. Being blessed requires you to go where the blessings can be found and God placed your blessings along the road called obedience. When you go off on your own road, God won't lose sight of you, you still belong to him, but you'll be missing out on the benefits he intends for you to have; the ones found along the road he set for you. If you find that your blessings are few and far between, you might want to make sure you're following his directions.

My Reflections and Responses:

_____

_____

_____

_____

_____

Date: _____   126

Psalms 119:9-11 *9 How can a young person live a clean life? By carefully reading the map of your Word. 10 I'm single-minded in pursuit of you; don't let me miss the road signs you've posted. 11 I've banked your promises in the vault of my heart so I won't sin myself bankrupt.*

How can a young person, who hasn't had time or opportunity to go through the process that God usually requires before giving the gift of wisdom, live a clean life? There is a shortcut for living that kind of life. Read God's Word and do exactly what it says in simple obedience without requiring complete understanding. Understanding might or might not come later, but in the meantime you'll be accumulating his promises, directions, knowledge and inspiration in your heart. Obedience doesn't require understanding but it does require a single-minded pursuit of him.

My Reflections and Responses:

_____

_____

_____

_____

_____

_____

Date: _____   127

Psalms 119:12-16 *12 Be blessed, GOD; train me in your ways of wise living. 13 I'll transfer to my lips all the counsel that comes from your mouth; 14 I delight far more in what you tell me about living than in gathering a pile of riches. 15 I ponder every morsel of wisdom from you, I attentively watch how you've done it. 16 I relish everything you've told me of life, I won't forget a word of it.*

Your relationship with God is meant to include much more than just asking him for stuff. Talk to him, listen to him, watch what he does and learn how to live life by following his lead. Accumulate wealth and property if that pleases you but don't forget where it all comes from and where it all goes when you're gone so you never forget what's really important. Your relationship with God should expand your life, not take away from it. Invite him into every aspect of your life, live a full and interesting one and enjoy all the gifts and talents he has blessed you with. Just stay away from going anywhere or doing anything you would be uncomfortable inviting him to participate in.

My Reflections and Responses:

_____

_____

_____

_____

Date: _____   128

Psalms 119:25-32 *25 I'm feeling terrible — I couldn't feel worse! Get me on my feet again. You promised, remember? 26 When I told my story, you responded; train me well in your deep wisdom. 27 Help me understand these things inside and out so I can ponder your miracle-wonders. 28 My sad life's dilapidated, a falling-down barn; build me up again by your Word. 29 Barricade the road that goes Nowhere; grace me with your clear revelation. 30 I choose the true road to Somewhere, I post your road signs at every curve and corner. 31 I grasp and cling to whatever you tell me; GOD, don't let me down! 32 I'll run the course you lay out for me if you'll just show me how.*

There's a road that goes nowhere and one that goes somewhere. The one that goes nowhere is easy to find. Just start walking on your own and you're bound to find it. It goes on and on but when you get to where you're going, you won't have gotten anywhere; your life will still be a disaster. You'll never accidently stumble onto the road that goes somewhere; you have to deliberately choose it. God's Word contains the map to that road, and a relationship with him reveals its mysteries, enabling and empowering you to clearly understand and follow his directions.

My Reflections and Responses:

_____

_____

_____

Date: _____   129

Psalms 119:33-37 *33 GOD, teach me lessons for living so I can stay the course. 34 Give me insight so I can do what you tell me — my whole life one long, obedient response. 35 Guide me down the road of your commandments; I love traveling this freeway! 36 Give me a bent for your words of wisdom, and not for piling up loot. 37 Divert my eyes from toys and trinkets, invigorate me on the pilgrim way.*

You can want to live right, and try with all your might, but that isn't enough. You can't do it without the lessons that only God can teach you. You can't even obey him without the insight that only he can supply. He's the only one who can give you the strength and desire to seek his, not the world's ways. Go to him, submit to him, ask and he will give you everything you need to be able to chose him; then chose him again and again for the rest of your life.

My Reflections and Responses:

_____

_____

_____

_____

_____

_____

_____

Date: _____   130

Psalms 119:44-46 *44 Oh, I'll guard with my life what you've revealed to me, guard it now, guard it ever; 45 And I'll stride freely through wide open spaces as I look for your truth and your wisdom; 46 Then I'll tell the world what I find, speak out boldly in public, unembarrassed.*

Once you've received revelation from God, nothing else will ever compare. Everything else you thought you knew only pointed you in the right direction; his Word, alive and life giving, is your destination. You will instantly develop a desire for more and will never be satisfied with anything less. What he speaks to you will be so wonderful and powerful, you'll want to share it over and over with everyone you see.

My Reflections and Responses:

_____

_____

_____

_____

_____

_____

_____

_____

Date: _____

Psalms 119:62-64 *62 I get up in the middle of the night to thank you; your decisions are so right, so true — I can't wait till morning! 63 I'm a friend and companion of all who fear you, of those committed to living by your rules. 64 Your love, GOD, fills the earth! Train me to live by your counsel.*

If you find yourself awake in the middle of the night, instead of worrying about missing out on a little sleep, why not talk to God; he's always awake and ready for conversation. You probably don't want to bring up all of the problems you struggle with during the day; you'll never get back to sleep. Try thanking him and praising him for all the wonderful advice he's given you. Talk to him about all the good things he's provided and the mercy he's shown you and your family. If you fall back to sleep, that's fine; if you don't, it will be the best sleep loss you've had in a long time. When you get up in the morning, hang out with people who love and obey God; come nighttime, you'll have much less to lose sleep over.

My Reflections and Responses:

_____

_____

_____

_____

_____

Date: _____   132

Psalms 119:73-76 *73 With your very own hands you formed me; now breathe your wisdom over me so I can understand you. 74 When they see me waiting, expecting your Word, those who fear you will take heart and be glad. 75 I can see now, GOD, that your decisions are right; your testing has taught me what's true and right. 76 Oh, love me — and right now! — hold me tight! just the way you promised.*

The one who created you is the one whose wisdom you need. You can listen to every preacher that comes along, read every book ever written, even memorize the Bible cover to cover, but until he breathes wisdom over you, it's all just knowledge; you won't be any wiser, just better informed. If it hasn't happened yet, you haven't asked or aren't quite ready for it; don't run out ahead of his wisdom, wait expectantly. While you wait, go ahead and do all of those other things, they are good to do, just not sufficient. Don't be upset if you have to go through some testing along the way; it's God's way of showing you what you don't know, what you already know, and what you still have to learn, which is probably quite a lot. Don't feel stupid when you fail; be grateful that he is taking the time to give you a private lesson.

My Reflections and Responses:

_____

_____

_____

Date: _____

Psalms 119:89-93 *89 What you say goes, GOD, and stays, as permanent as the heavens. 90 Your truth never goes out of fashion; it's as up-to-date as the earth when the sun comes up. 91 Your Word and truth are dependable as ever; that's what you ordered — you set the earth going. 92 If your revelation hadn't delighted me so, I would have given up when the hard times came. 93 But I'll never forget the advice you gave me; you saved my life with those wise words.*

Have you ever read a ten year old newspaper, medical book, science text, or fashion magazine? You'll be amazed at how many things we absolutely depended on to be true, accurate and up-to-date are now found to be completely false, obsolete and totally out of fashion. Go back a hundred years and you'll have a hard time finding any useful information at all. Now read God's Word and try to find something, anything, that doesn't apply to your life ten years ago, now, and ten, twenty or one hundred years from now. You can count on his Word to always be accurate and never changing. If you are in need of new revelation, read the same Word you read yesterday and you will find fresh insight for today; it's called the living Word of God and is just what you need for every occasion.

My Reflections and Responses:

_____

_____

Date: _____   134

Psalms 119:97-100 *97 Oh, how I love all you've revealed; I reverently ponder it all the day long. 98 Your commands give me an edge on my enemies; they never become obsolete. 99 I've even become smarter than my teachers since I've pondered and absorbed your counsel. 100 I've become wiser than the wise old sages simply by doing what you tell me.*

F ormal education is a wonderful way of benefiting from a world of knowledge and information that you will never have the opportunity to experience personally. Study and learn all you can from anyone who knows something you don't and is willing to share it with you. If you want to be wise beyond your years, your experiences and your education, go to God for wisdom that can't be taught or learned but only revealed. Listen to him, immerse yourself in his ways and just do what he tells you. Because he is the creator of all things, he is the knower of all things and is always in a sharing mood.

My Reflections and Responses:

_____

_____

_____

_____

_____

_____

Date: _____

Psalms 119:105-107 *105 By your words I can see where I'm going; they throw a beam of light on my dark path. 106 I've committed myself and I'll never turn back from living by your righteous order. 107 Everything's falling apart on me, GOD; put me together again with your Word.*

Dedicating yourself to obeying and following God doesn't mean your life won't keep falling apart. Houses get old, cars get old, bodies get old and eventually wear out and fall apart. Living for him and walking by the light of his Word does mean he will keep putting you back together as many times as necessary and you won't be spending most of your time fumbling around in the dark doing needless harm to yourself. His Word gives you light and life because he is his Word.

My Reflections and Responses:

_____

_____

_____

_____

_____

_____

_____

_____

Date: _____   136

Psalms 119:124-125 *124 Let your love dictate how you deal with me; teach me from your textbook on life. 125 I'm your servant — help me understand what that means, the inner meaning of your instructions.*

The last thing you want is for God's justice and judgment to dictate how he deals with you. Pray that his love, mercy and grace dictate his actions toward you. While you're praying, don't forget to pray for your enemies as well as your friends. Be very cautious about praying for justice and judgment; the standards you set for others might end up being applied to you. Ask God what it really means to be his servant; he's very good to his servants and will take care of all that justice and judgment stuff so you can concentrate on love.

My Reflections and Responses:

_____

_____

_____

_____

_____

_____

_____

Date: _____   137

Psalms 119:129-130 *129 Every word you give me is a miracle word — how could I help but obey? 130 Break open your words, let the light shine out, let ordinary people see the meaning.*

Poetry is beautiful, melodic, inspiring and entertaining but poetry is not miracle. If you read God's Word as poetry, you'll enjoy it and probably learn from it but you won't notice any miracles in your life because of it. For the light to shine out of his Word and cause miraculous things to start happen in your life, he has to reveal its true meaning and you have to be willing and prepared to receive it. His Word is the living Word but only when he breathes life into it. Ask God to open his Word to you.

My Reflections and Responses:

_____

_____

_____

_____

_____

_____

_____

_____

Date: _____   138

Psalms 121:1-2 *1 I look up to the mountains; does my strength come from mountains? 2 No, my strength comes from GOD, who made heaven, and earth, and mountains.*

When you're feeling small and insignificant, look up to the tallest formation that exists on earth, the mountain. You can either begin to feel even more minute and lost in this gigantic universe, or you can remind yourself that the one who created that mountain, the heaven, earth and everything in-between cares so much for you that he knows every hair on your head, every move you make. His children are of far greater value to him than all the rest of his creation put together. How much more significant do you need to be?

My Reflections and Responses:

_____

_____

_____

_____

_____

_____

_____

_____

Date: _____

Psalms 121:5-8 *5 GOD's your Guardian, right at your side to protect you — 6 Shielding you from sunstroke, sheltering you from moonstroke. 7 GOD guards you from every evil, he guards your very life. 8 He guards you when you leave and when you return, he guards you now, he guards you always.*

With God protecting you day and night, coming and going, now and forever, what more do you need to feel safe and secure? If you're feeling afraid, it can't be because you're really in danger; remember, you have God watching over you. Feelings are powerful and important but don't get them mixed up with fact. Feelings aren't good or bad, right or wrong; they happen as a result of what you tell yourself. If you tell yourself you're in danger, you'll be afraid. If you tell yourself you're safe, you'll feel secure, whether you really are or not. If you want your feelings to reflect reality, make sure you tell yourself the truth; you can always do your fact check in God's Word.

My Reflections and Responses:

_____

_____

_____

_____

_____

Date: _____   140

Psalms 127:1-2 *1 If GOD doesn't build the house, the builders only build shacks. If GOD doesn't guard the city, the night watchman might as well nap. 2 It's useless to rise early and go to bed late, and work your worried fingers to the bone. Don't you know he enjoys giving rest to those he loves?*

If you're exhausted, working yourself to death working for God, you're not following his plan for your life. He never intended for your life to be all work and no rest, relaxation or play. You might be carrying out his assignment all right, but you've undoubtedly added quite a few things to your to-do list that you or someone else has decided God needs help with. He'll get his work done just fine without using up and wearing out the ones he loves. He created a twenty-fore hour day in which to eat, sleep, work, play, love a partner, raise a family, worship, pray and serve him with time to spare for dreaming. He could have easily created a thirty-six hour day but he didn't. If you're running out of time, you're trying to do too much.

My Reflections and Responses:

_____

_____

_____

_____

_____

Date: _____   141

Psalms 130:3-4 *3 If you, GOD, kept records on wrongdoings, who would stand a chance? 4 As it turns out, forgiveness is your habit, and that's why you're worshiped.*

We don't worship him because we are afraid not to; we do it because we love him so much we can't help ourselves. If we had to carry around a long list of our past sins, we wouldn't have the strength or enthusiasm to lift our hands in praise. It's his extraordinary love and incredible willingness to forgive, made possible through his son Jesus, that creates an overwhelming desire to love him back, serve him forever, and worship him for eternity. A habit is something you've done over and over so many times, it becomes automatic. Be like your heavenly Father and make forgiveness your habit.

My Reflections and Responses:

_____

_____

_____

_____

_____

_____

_____

Date: _____   142

Psalms 131:1-2 *1 GOD, I'm not trying to rule the roost, I don't want to be king of the mountain. I haven't meddled where I have no business or fantasized grandiose plans. 2 I've kept my feet on the ground, I've cultivated a quiet heart. Like a baby content in its mother's arms, my soul is a baby content.*

A baby snuggled in his mother's arms has no need to be the boss, control his environment, or make a name for himself; he's right where he wants to be and is content being cared for and protected by the one who loves him. Love is not competitive; it's freely given and freely accepted like that mother and her baby. Don't get too worked up over what you're going to accomplish in life, for yourself or for God. Your sole finds its home in the arms of God; everything else will come and go and eventually go away, but your relationship with him will last forever; that's something to really be impressed with.

My Reflections and Responses:

_____

_____

_____

_____

_____

_____

Date: _____

Psalms 139:1-6 *1 GOD, investigate my life; get all the facts firsthand. 2 I'm an open book to you; even from a distance, you know what I'm thinking. 3 You know when I leave and when I get back; I'm never out of your sight. 4 You know everything I'm going to say before I start the first sentence. 5 I look behind me and you're there, then up ahead and you're there, too — your reassuring presence, coming and going. 6 This is too much, too wonderful — I can't take it all in!*

Have you ever been loved by someone and wondered how they'd feel if they knew the real you, inside and out? You never have to worry about that with God; you are totally transparent and thoroughly known, inside and out, forwards, backwards, past, present, future and completely loved. Do your best for him because you love him, but don't worry too much about your efforts being good enough; when you become a member of his family, your love is what he really wants and his love is what you already have.

My Reflections and Responses:

_____

_____

_____

_____

_____

_____

Date: _____   144

Psalms 139:23-24 *23 Investigate my life, O God, find out everything about me; Cross-examine and test me, get a clear picture of what I'm about; 24 See for yourself whether I've done anything wrong — then guide me on the road to eternal life.*

It shouldn't be a scary thing to invite God to investigate your life and test you. Of course there are going to be parts of that test that you fail. It wouldn't be a very good test if it didn't point out where you still need help. Remember, God loves you and fully intends for you to pass the final exam; he's not trying to trip you up, only expose those areas of your life that aren't quite up to eternal standards yet. It's not like he doesn't already know everything about you, but he's waiting for you to invite his participation in your transformation.

My Reflections and Responses:

_____

_____

_____

_____

_____

_____

_____

Date: _____   145

Psalms 143:7-8 *7 Hurry with your answer, GOD! I'm nearly at the end of my rope. Don't turn away; don't ignore me! That would be certain death. 8 If you wake me each morning with the sound of your loving voice, I'll go to sleep each night trusting in you. Point out the road I must travel; I'm all ears, all eyes before you.*

I n his great wisdom, God created you with a short attention span. Even if you clearly hear his voice, by tomorrow, you might begin to forget exactly what he said and even start to doubt that it was he who said it. If he wakes you each morning with the sound of his voice, you'll probably make it through the day and go to sleep at night still trusting him. By tomorrow morning you'll need another word, another touch, another revelation from him or by nighttime you might already have begun to lose your way. It takes a daily talk to have a daily walk with him. Watch and listen to everything God has to say every day. He sent his son Jesus, not only to point out the way to you, but to be the Way for you.

My Reflections and Responses:

_____

_____

_____

_____

_____

Date: _____   146

Psalms 146:3-5 *3 Don't put your life in the hands of experts who know nothing of life, of salvation life. 4 Mere humans don't have what it takes; when they die, their projects die with them. 5 Instead, get help from the God of Jacob, put your hope in GOD and know real blessing!*

God did not isolate us from believers or unbelievers. We were not created to live totally independent lives, uninvolved and untouched by others; looking to him only for companionship and help. Believers will be encouraged and lifted up by your involvement in their lives and the only exposure to the Lord some unbelievers will ever have will be through their interaction with you. Participate fully, help and accept help from others, but know their limitations; don't put your life in anyone's hands except God's. He's the only one you can totally trust in every situation to completely understand and abundantly supply exactly what you need.

My Reflections and Responses:

_____

_____

_____

_____

_____

Date: _____

Psalms 150 Hallelujah! Praise God in his holy house of worship, praise him under the open skies; 2 Praise him for his acts of power, praise him for his magnificent greatness; 3 Praise with a blast on the trumpet, praise by strumming soft strings; 4 Praise him with castanets and dance, praise him with banjo and flute; 5 Praise him with cymbals and a big bass drum, praise him with fiddles and mandolin. 6 Let every living, breathing creature praise GOD! Hallelujah!

Praise God in every way you can, with everything you have, for everything he does for you and is to you, which is everything of any eternal significance. Be sure that your praise and worship far exceed your requests. There is nothing you can think to ask for that he isn't already aware of, nothing you can tell him that he doesn't already know, so concentrate most of your time and effort on what pleases him the most; the only unique, one-of-a-kind gift that you can ever offer to the one who has everything; your love. Hallelujah! Hallelujah! Hallelujah!

My Reflections and Responses:

_____

_____

_____

_____

_____

Date: _____   148

Proverbs 1:1-2 *1 These are the wise sayings of Solomon, David's son, Israel's king — 2 Written down so we'll know how to live well and right, to understand what life means and where it's going*

It's not God's intent that we live a life of confusion. He wants us to live a good life, knowing why we're here and where we're going. It's when we look to ourselves for the meaning of life that we get all turned around and mixed up. He has revealed it all through his word. Sometimes it jumps out at us and sometimes we have to search a bit, but it's all right there waiting for our desire to find it.

My Reflections and Responses:

_____

_____

_____

_____

_____

_____

_____

_____

_____

Date: _____

Proverbs 1:3-6 *3 A manual for living, for learning what's right and just and fair; 4 To teach the inexperienced the ropes and give our young people a grasp on reality. 5 There's something here also for seasoned men and women, 6 still a thing or two for the experienced to learn — Fresh wisdom to probe and penetrate, the rhymes and reasons of wise men and women.*

His word, from proverb to beatitude, is simple enough for a child to grasp and profound enough to challenge the wisest among us. Whatever the question, it's the answer. Because it's the Living Word, the same scripture that answered your question yesterday, might be the perfect answer to an entirely different question today. That's the mystery and majesty of the Word of God.

My Reflections and Responses:

_____

_____

_____

_____

_____

_____

_____

_____

_____

Date: _____   150

Proverbs 1:10,15-19 *10 Dear friend, if bad companions tempt you, don't go along with them...15 Oh, friend, don't give them a second look; don't listen to them for a minute. 16 They're racing to a very bad end, hurrying to ruin everything they lay hands on. 17 Nobody robs a bank with everyone watching, 18 Yet that's what these people are doing — they're doing themselves in. 19 When you grab all you can get, that's what happens: the more you get, the less you are.*

When bad companions tempt you, they make it sound so reasonable and exciting. Surround yourself with bad people and they seem like the majority. Step back and you can see that they are destroying themselves and everyone who goes along with them. Stick around and you'll end up with a hand full of trinkets and a life that means nothing.

My Reflections and Responses:

_____

_____

_____

_____

_____

_____

_____

Date: _____   151

Proverbs 1:27-28 *27 What if the roof falls in, and your whole life goes to pieces? What if catastrophe strikes and there's nothing to show for your life but rubble and ashes? 28 You'll need me then. You'll call for me, but don't expect an answer. No matter how hard you look, you won't find me.*

Wisdom seems unnecessarily cumbersome when everything is going right. It stops you from doing whatever you want, without regard for the consequences. It sobers you up and sets you straight when you'd rather have the freedom to wonder off the path a bit. But what happens when things start falling apart? You'll wish you had wisdom in a hurry, but you won't find it. Wisdom isn't fast food, available at a moment's notice; it's a slow simmering stew that takes as long as it takes, and won't be hurried.

My Reflections and Responses:

_____

_____

_____

_____

_____

_____

_____

Date: _____   152

Proverbs 1:29-33 29 *"Because you hated Knowledge and had nothing to do with the Fear-of-GOD, 30 Because you wouldn't take my advice and brushed aside all my offers to train you, 31 Well, you've made your bed — now lie in it; you wanted your own way — now, how do you like it? 32 Don't you see what happens, you simpletons, you idiots? Carelessness kills; complacency is murder. 33 First pay attention to me, and then relax. Now you can take it easy — you're in good hands."*

There will be plenty of time to relax and take it easy but first things first. Submit yourself to the discipline of education, and make getting your life right with God your first priority, then you'll know when to work and when to rest. A baker, in such a hurry to eat the cake that he ignores the recipe and bakes the ingredients before taking the time to combine them, will get a mess that will never come together into something edible.

My Reflections and Responses:

_____

_____

_____

_____

_____

_____

_____

Date: _____   153

Proverbs 2:3-5 *3 That's right — if you make Insight your priority, and won't take no for an answer, 4 Searching for it like a prospector panning for gold, like an adventurer on a treasure hunt, 5 Believe me, before you know it Fear-of-GOD will be yours; you'll have come upon the Knowledge of God.*

If you're determined to go anywhere and do anything to find insight, understanding, knowledge, wisdom and truth, what you will find, sooner than later, is God. All those things you were looking for can only be found in him, and it doesn't take a lifetime to find him, but it does take eternity to experience him.

My Reflections and Responses:

_____

_____

_____

_____

_____

_____

_____

_____

_____

_____

Date: _____   154

Proverbs 2:6-8 *6 And here's why: GOD gives out Wisdom free, is plainspoken in Knowledge and Understanding. 7 He's a rich mine of Common Sense for those who live well, a personal bodyguard to the candid and sincere. 8 He keeps his eye on all who live honestly, and pays special attention to his loyally committed ones.*

If you look for knowledge and understanding, if you're committed to God and to living an honest sincere life, you will not only find what you're looking for, but wisdom will be your free bonus. Because God is truth, if you live your life in any other way, you remove yourself from his presence. He gave you a free will so he'll let you, but his desire is to always be with you and look after you. Why would anyone deprive themselves of such a wonderful blessing?

My Reflections and Responses:

_____

_____

_____

_____

_____

_____

_____

Date: _____   155

Proverbs 2:9-15 *9 So now you can pick out what's true and fair, find all the good trails! 10 Lady Wisdom will be your close friend, and Brother Knowledge your pleasant companion. 11 Good Sense will scout ahead for danger, Insight will keep an eye out for you. 12 They'll keep you from making wrong turns, or following the bad directions 13 Of those who are lost themselves and can't tell a trail from a tumbleweed, 14 These losers who make a game of evil and throw parties to celebrate perversity, 15 Traveling paths that go nowhere, wandering in a maze of detours and dead ends.*

Walk with losers, listen to their directions, and you'll all end up the same place, nowhere. Don't think you can spend your life with losers and be a winner. Walk with God and wisdom, knowledge, good sense and insight will be your companions. They will help you make your decisions and will show you the way. Instead of the dead end that goes nowhere, you'll end up in eternity with all of God's loyal children.

My Reflections and Responses:

_____

_____

_____

_____

_____

_____

Date: _____   156

Proverbs 3:3-4 *3 Don't lose your grip on Love and Loyalty. Tie them around your neck; carve their initials on your heart. 4 Earn a reputation for living well in God's eyes and the eyes of the people.*

L ove and loyalty go together. Love that you can't count on, that isn't faithful and dependable, isn't worth much. Disappointment and pain are the fruit of that kind of love, which might be a momentary feeling but isn't really love at all.

My Reflections and Responses:

_____

_____

_____

_____

_____

_____

_____

_____

_____

_____

_____

Date: _____

Proverbs 3:5-8 *5 Trust GOD from the bottom of your heart; don't try to figure out everything on your own. 6 Listen for GOD's voice in everything you do, everywhere you go; he's the one who will keep you on track. 7 Don't assume that you know it all. Run to GOD! Run from evil! 8 Your body will glow with health*

If you really trust God from the bottom of your heart, you wouldn't think of trying to figure out everything on your own. Assuming that you know everything, or can figure it out without any help, is the height of arrogance, and a vast simplification of the enormity of God's magnificent creation. Stick with the creator and it's quite simple; try to go it alone and before long you will be totally overwhelmed, and lost beyond imagination.

My Reflections and Responses:

_____

_____

_____

_____

_____

_____

_____

_____

Date: _____   158

Proverbs 3:9-12 *9 Honor GOD with everything you own; give him the first and the best. 10 Your barns will burst, your wine vats will brim over. 11 But don't, dear friend, resent GOD's discipline; don't sulk under his loving correction. 12 It's the child he loves that GOD corrects; a father's delight is behind all this.*

It's sometimes easer to give God your best than to accept his best in return. His loving correction is a part of his best. A father, who doesn't lovingly correct his children, isn't giving them his best and doesn't really love them. God loves you far too much to just turn you lose and let you destroy your life for lack of instruction. If you insist, he will of course, let you ignore his intervention for a time, but fortunately, no matter how many steps you take away from him, it's always only one step back into his loving care.

My Reflections and Responses:

_____

_____

_____

_____

_____

_____

_____

Date: _____   159

Proverbs 3:19-20 *19 With Lady Wisdom, GOD formed Earth; with Madame Insight, he raised Heaven. 20 They knew when to signal rivers and springs to the surface, and dew to descend from the night skies.*

What magnificent artistry, perfect symmetry, and wonderful balance God's creation is. He draws life giving water up from the depths of earth and down from the heights of Heaven to form a habitat for his favorite creation, man. He gave us earth to enjoy and Heaven to hope for. Either would be less without the other. Together, they form a perfect setting for eternity.

My Reflections and Responses:

_____

_____

_____

_____

_____

_____

_____

_____

_____

_____

_____

Date: _____   160

Proverbs 3:25-26 *25 No need to panic over alarms or surprises, or predictions that doomsday's just around the corner, 26 Because GOD will be right there with you; he'll keep you safe and sound.*

With God beside you, there is no such thing as doomsday, and alarms or surprises are just opportunities for God to show off a little. Relax and enjoy the most exciting ride of your life with complete confidence that he will keep you safe.

My Reflections and Responses:

_____

_____

_____

_____

_____

_____

_____

_____

_____

_____

_____

Date: _____   161

Proverbs 3:27 *Never walk away from someone who deserves help; your hand is God's hand for that person.*

Examine your hand closely, pay attention to all the things your hand has done. Who has it helped, who has it harmed, who has it comforted, or not. Now look again even more closely because you're looking at God's hand. What would his hand do? Do that, and never look at your hand again as just another hand.

My Reflections and Responses:

_____

_____

_____

_____

_____

_____

_____

_____

_____

_____

Date: _____   162

Proverbs 3:30-32 *30 Don't walk around with a chip on your shoulder, always spoiling for a fight. 31 Don't try to be like those who shoulder their way through life. Why be a bully? 32 "Why not?" you say. Because GOD can't stand twisted souls. It's the straightforward who get his respect.*

Even asking the question "Why not be a bully?" means you haven't got it yet; you think life is all about getting and all about you. If you twist anything enough it makes a complete circle and ends up right back where it started, nothing gained, nothing accomplished. That's even true of a twisted soul. It ends up with nothing but itself, alone and empty. If everything is always about you, you end up with only you, just like the bully. If you pour your life into others, you'll end up with others who do the same. You'll all end up full and fulfilled.

My Reflections and Responses:

_____

_____

_____

_____

_____

_____

_____

Date: _____   163

Proverbs 4:16-17 *16 Evil people are restless unless they're making trouble; They can't get a good night's sleep unless they've made life miserable for somebody. 17 Perversity is their food and drink, violence their drug of choice.*

Evil can be every bit as addictive as alcohol or drugs. Practice evil long enough and you'll find yourself dependent on the high you get from it. Normal life, or even a good life, will seem bland and boring compared to the adrenalin rush you get when you break all the rules. What you continually repeat in your life will eventually become a habit; make it a good one not a bad one.

My Reflections and Responses:

_____

_____

_____

_____

_____

_____

_____

_____

_____

Date: _____   164

Proverbs 4:18-19 *18 The ways of right-living people glow with light; the longer they live, the brighter they shine. 19 But the road of wrongdoing gets darker and darker — travelers can't see a thing; they fall flat on their faces.*

The "ways" of right-living people are their habits, conduct, customs, and traditions. "Ways" have a way of growing and becoming more established with time; all the better to reflect the glory of the Lord. That must be why they shine. Wrongdoers travel a road that leads them away from the light so their world just gets darker not brighter. Speaking of bright, if you really want to feel stupid, try doing all the ordinary things you do, but do them in the dark.

My Reflections and Responses:

_____

_____

_____

_____

_____

_____

_____

_____

Date: _____

Proverbs 4:23-24 *23 Keep vigilant watch over your heart; that's where life starts. 24 Don't talk out of both sides of your mouth; avoid careless banter, white lies, and gossip.*

Your heart is where life starts and also where it ends. Out of your heart come the words you speak. Speak words of life, not death.

My Reflections and Responses:

_____

_____

_____

_____

_____

_____

_____

_____

_____

_____

_____

_____

_____

Date: _____

Proverbs 5:10-14 *10 Why should you allow strangers to take advantage of you? Why be exploited by those who care nothing for you? 11 You don't want to end your life full of regrets, nothing but sin and bones, 12 Saying, "Oh, why didn't I do what they told me? Why did I reject a disciplined life? 13 Why didn't I listen to my mentors, or take my teachers seriously? 14 My life is ruined! I haven't one blessed thing to show for my life!"*

L iving a life of being used and abused isn't a righteous life, it's a wasted life. It's your choice whether you listen to those who would exploit you or those who would exhort you.

My Reflections and Responses:

_____

_____

_____

_____

_____

_____

_____

_____

_____

_____

Date: _____

Proverbs 5:15-16 *15 Do you know the saying, "Drink from your own rain barrel, draw water from your own spring-fed well"? 16 It's true. Otherwise, you may one day come home and find your barrel empty and your well polluted.*

Fatefulness inspires fatefulness. Loyalty inspires loyalty. Disrespect your spouse by looking elsewhere for your intimacies and ecstasies and you not only weaken the bond that holds you to your partner, you also weaken the bond that holds your partner to you. Even a longing glance at someone other than the one God gave you, begins to erode and dilute the powerful connection that God intended to be second only to your relationship with him.

My Reflections and Responses:

_____

_____

_____

_____

_____

_____

_____

_____

Date: _____   168

Proverbs 5:18-20 *18 Enjoy the wife you married as a young man! 19 Lovely as an angel, beautiful as a rose — don't ever quit taking delight in her body. Never take her love for granted! 20 Why would you trade enduring intimacies for cheap thrills with a whore? For dalliance with a promiscuous stranger?*

A parent embraces their newborn baby and beholds the most beautiful sight they've ever seen. They wouldn't trade that wrinkly, wiggly, stinky thing for anything in the world. As time goes on, that baby transforms into a toddler, child, teen, young adult, and eventually, if that parent lives long enough, a wrinkly, stinky old person. Through all of those stages of life, a parent's love doesn't start getting old and worn out; it continues to grow stronger and stronger with each life experience shared with that child. The love between a parent and child is heart to heart and the heart has an infinite capacity to love. Who would ever consider trading their own child in for a smarter, more attractive and interesting one? There is no such thing to a loving parent. Marriage is intended to be like that.

My Reflections and Responses:

_____

_____

_____

Date: _____   169

Proverbs 5:21 *Mark well that GOD doesn't miss a move you make; he's aware of every step you take.*

The realization that God knows every step you take, can be quite frightening. Your first thought might be of all those things you'd just as soon he not notice. Think again; his love for you doesn't turn off and on each time you take a wrong step or a right one. He knows each move you make because you are that important to him. Of course he'll correct you when you need it, but he's there to protect you when you need it also. You never have to be all alone and on your own. He's not always in your face, he'll give you plenty of space, but don't think he doesn't care, and don't forget he's always there.

My Reflections and Responses:

_____

_____

_____

_____

_____

_____

_____

_____

Date: _____   170

Proverbs 6:16-19 *16 Here are six things GOD hates, and one more that he loathes with a passion: 17 eyes that are arrogant, a tongue that lies, hands that murder the innocent, 18 a heart that hatches evil plots, feet that race down a wicked track, 19 a mouth that lies under oath, a troublemaker in the family.*

Why would God loath "troublemakers in the family" even more than he hates the other six sins? We're living in troubled times. It's been that way since Adam and Eve left the garden, and it's only getting worse. God knew we'd need a refuge, a place of safety where we could go when the world got to be too much to take. God designed the family to be our sanctuary city, a place where we could drop our guard, rest in peace, and know that we would always be loved and accepted, even on those rare occasions when we weren't being the most lovable and acceptable. A troublemaker in the family destroys the safety of that sanctuary and even worse, corrupts one of God's most exquisite designs, relationships. The devil got kicked out of heaven for causing trouble in the family, along with all the other angles that refused to get along. God takes that kind of betrayal very seriously.

My Reflections and Responses:

_____

_____

Date: _____   171

Proverbs 6:27-29 *27 Can you build a fire in your lap and not burn your pants? 28 Can you walk barefoot on hot coals and not get blisters? 29 It's the same when you have sex with your neighbor's wife: Touch her and you'll pay for it. No excuses.*

Ll three are voluntary acts and all three have consequences. The fire doesn't care if you thought you were fireproof and the husband doesn't care if you thought you loved his wife or she loved you. Consequences don't take ignorance into consideration and they aren't impressed with good intentions. If you decide to take the risk, remember all the others who will pay the price, not just the two of you.

My Reflections and Responses:

_____

_____

_____

_____

_____

_____

_____

_____

_____

Date: _____   172

Proverbs 6:32-33 *32 Adultery is a brainless act, soul-destroying, self-destructive; 33 Expect a bloody nose, a black eye, and a reputation ruined for good.*

Adultery is never the logical act of an intelligent person; it's either an entirely emotional act that requires sacrificing everything else for a feeling, or the incredibly arrogant act of a person who just doesn't care about anyone else, or both. Adultery seems to either cause or reveal stupidity, I'm not sure which.

My Reflections and Responses:

_____

_____

_____

_____

_____

_____

_____

_____

_____

_____

_____

Date: _____   173

Proverbs 6:34-35 *34 For jealousy detonates rage in a cheated husband; wild for revenge, he won't make allowances. 35 Nothing you say or pay will make it all right; neither bribes nor reason will satisfy him.*

You can't restore someone else's relationship once you've destroyed it. You can't even restore your own once you've betrayed it. You can have your relationship with God restored by going to him and repenting. After that, try to make amends where you can, and pray that God will heal the wounds that you've caused. You'll always get another chance with God; others might or might not be so generous.

My Reflections and Responses:

_____

_____

_____

_____

_____

_____

_____

_____

_____

Date: _____   174

Proverbs 8:10-11 *10 Prefer my life-disciplines over chasing after money, and God-knowledge over a lucrative career. 11 For Wisdom is better than all the trappings of wealth; nothing you could wish for holds a candle to her.*

Trappings are the frills, the accessories, the extras. God created people as the expression and recipient of his love. His relationship with his people, his ever expanding family, is always the main event. Everything else is extra. With wisdom that comes from knowing God, you won't bother chasing after the extras, you'll concern yourself with the main event, relationship with God first and others after that.

My Reflections and Responses:

_____

_____

_____

_____

_____

_____

_____

_____

_____

Date: _____   175

Proverbs 8:12 *"I am Lady Wisdom, and I live next to Sanity;*
Knowledge and Discretion live just down the street.

G o into any neighborhood and you'll notice right away that there are no mansions in a poor neighborhood, and you won't find any run down shacks in the million dollar community. Wisdom lives in an exclusive neighborhood with sanity, knowledge and discretion. If you want wisdom, don't waste your time looking in just any old place. You won't stumble on it accidently. You have to go looking where it's likely to be found.

My Reflections and Responses:

_____

_____

_____

_____

_____

_____

_____

_____

_____

Date: _____   176

Proverbs 8:17-19 *17 I love those who love me; those who look for me find me. 18 Wealth and Glory accompany me — also substantial Honor and a Good Name. 19 My benefits are worth more than a big salary, even a very big salary; the returns on me exceed any imaginable bonus.*

No one is born with wisdom; no one inherits it. You can't accidently stumble on to it, and if you have it, you can't give it away. You can give someone else information or knowledge, but wisdom is individually acquired. You have to love it and intentionally look for it and you will find it. Wisdom comes as a result of acquiring knowledge, gaining understanding, and applying discretion over a substantial period of time. If you have it, you won't misuse it; if you do, you've already lost it.

My Reflections and Responses:

_____

_____

_____

_____

_____

_____

_____

Date: _____

Proverbs 8:22-31 *22 "GOD sovereignly made me — the first, the basic — before he did anything else. 23 I was brought into being a long time ago, well before Earth got its start. 24 I arrived on the scene before Ocean, yes, even before Springs and Rivers and Lakes. 25 Before Mountains were sculpted and Hills took shape, I was already there, newborn; 26 Long before GOD stretched out Earth's Horizons, and tended to the minute details of Soil and Weather, 27 And set Sky firmly in place, I was there. When he mapped and gave borders to wild Ocean, 28 built the vast vault of Heaven, and installed the fountains that fed Ocean, 29 When he drew a boundary for Sea, posted a sign that said, NO TRESPASSING, And then staked out Earth's foundations, 30 I was right there with him, making sure everything fit. Day after day I was there, with my joyful applause, always enjoying his company, 31 Delighted with the world of things and creatures, happily celebrating the human family.*

God created wisdom before he made anything else. Without it, creation would be a collection of meaningless junk that doesn't fit together, and has no meaning, purpose or direction. A lack of wisdom must be how scientists came up with the chaos theory and rejected the reality of creation.

My Reflections and Responses:

_____

_____

_____

Date: _____   178

Proverbs 9:7-9 *7 If you reason with an arrogant cynic, you'll get slapped in the face; confront bad behavior and get a kick in the shins. 8 So don't waste your time on a scoffer; all you'll get for your pains is abuse. But if you correct those who care about life, that's different — they'll love you for it! 9 Save your breath for the wise — they'll be wiser for it; tell good people what you know — they'll profit from it.*

You can't turn a bad person into a good one with words. You can't educate someone who prefers to remain ignorant. Their condition isn't the result of a lack of information; it's a condition of the heart and an attitude of the mind. You can be good to them, and that generous act might create an opening for the Holy Spirit to begin working in their life, but don't think you can change them. Their willing response to the conviction of the Holy Spirit is the only thing that can bring about real change. You can offer to help, but if you're rejected, don't waste your time. They just need more time for life and the Holy Spirit to soften them up a bit before they're ready to respond. It might be next week, next month or ten years from now, but meanwhile you have better things to do and places to go.

My Reflections and Responses:

_____

_____

_____

Date: _____   179

Proverbs 9:10-12 *10 Skilled living gets its start in the Fear-of-GOD, insight into life from knowing a Holy God. 11 It's through me, Lady Wisdom, that your life deepens, and the years of your life ripen. 12 Live wisely and wisdom will permeate your life; mock life and life will mock you.*

There is no real truth, knowledge, insight or wisdom apart from God. He is the creator of everything, even wisdom. Because he is the creator of body, mind and spirit, earth, heaven, and the entire universe, apply your God knowledge to every aspect of your life, not just the "spiritual" part. There is an order to everything; nothing created is random or unintentional. To function within that order in the way God intended, requires knowledge of him and submission to his design.

My Reflections and Responses:

_____

_____

_____

_____

_____

_____

_____

_____

Date: _____   180

Proverbs 10:10 *An evasive eye is a sign of trouble ahead, but an open, face-to-face meeting results in peace.*

Peace requires two people, two families, two communities or even two countries to work out their differences. That can't happen if they avoid each other or the issue in dispute.

My Reflections and Responses:

_____

_____

_____

_____

_____

_____

_____

_____

_____

_____

_____

_____

_____

_____

Date: _____   181

Proverbs 10:13 *You'll find wisdom on the lips of a person of insight, but the shortsighted needs a slap in the face.*

A person with insight is able to see an issue from outside their own perspective and offer information which might be worth listening to. A shortsighted person is only able to see how something affects their own life at the moment; not a very helpful perspective for anyone else. They might need something abrupt to jar them out of their self-centered view and extend their sight beyond their own self interest.

My Reflections and Responses:

_____

_____

_____

_____

_____

_____

_____

_____

_____

_____

Date: _____   182

Proverbs 10:19 *The more talk, the less truth; the wise measure their words.*

The truth is usually straightforward and requires little explanation. If you, or anyone else, need a lot of words to get your point across, you might want to examine that point closely. A lie needs lots of words to hide behind; truth speaks for itself.

My Reflections and Responses:

_____

_____

_____

_____

_____

_____

_____

_____

_____

_____

_____

_____

Date: _____

Proverbs 10:20 *The speech of a good person is worth waiting for; the blabber of the wicked is worthless.*

The value of a person's words is determined by the worth of the person, not the eloquence of their delivery. The most inspiring, compelling speech isn't worth much if you can't trust the person giving it.

My Reflections and Responses:

_____

_____

_____

_____

_____

_____

_____

_____

_____

_____

_____

_____

Proverbs 10:21 The talk of a good person is rich fare for many, but chatterboxes die of an empty heart.

What a good person says adds value to other's lives and that adds value to their own. A chatterbox goes on and on about nothing and nothing is what they end up with.

My Reflections and Responses:

_____

_____

_____

_____

_____

_____

_____

_____

_____

_____

_____

_____

_____

_____

Date: _____

Proverbs 10:25 *When the storm is over, there's nothing left of the wicked; good people, firm on their rock foundation, aren't even fazed.*

Regardless of outward appearance, if you aren't attached to something lasting, you won't last. The biggest, strongest anchor is worthless as long as it remains in the boat. It's not its own strength but what it's attached to that keeps the boat secure.

My Reflections and Responses:

_____

_____

_____

_____

_____

_____

_____

_____

_____

_____

_____

Date: _____

Proverbs 10:30 *Good people last — they can't be moved; the wicked are here today, gone tomorrow.*

Good people seem to gather together. Because they genuinely care for others, the groups they form have substance and strength. Wicked people are only out for themselves. If they do occasionally form a "mob", it's quickly dispersed as each member's self-interest takes them in a different direction. Try dispersing a group made up of members who love each other and are united in a common cause.

My Reflections and Responses:

_____

_____

_____

_____

_____

_____

_____

_____

_____

_____

Date: _____   187

Proverbs 10:32 *The speech of a good person clears the air; the words of the wicked pollute it.*

I t might get discouraging at times to observe all the pollution that continually comes out of the mouths of the wicked, but imagine how bad it would get if good people weren't constantly clearing that polluted air with their words. When a good person speaks, they are actually cleaning up the environment.

My Reflections and Responses:

_____

_____

_____

_____

_____

_____

_____

_____

_____

_____

_____

Date: _____   188

Proverbs 11:4 *A thick bankroll is no help when life falls apart, but a principled life can stand up to the worst.*

Life falling apart rarely has anything to do with anything that money can fix. When a car breaks down or a house burns down, life hasn't fallen apart. If someone you love was in that house, that's when life starts to fall apart. Money can't fix that. Nothing can fix that, but a life built upon principles, core beliefs and love will get you through, just barely.

My Reflections and Responses:

_____

_____

_____

_____

_____

_____

_____

_____

_____

_____

Date: _____

Proverbs 11:12 Mean-spirited slander is heartless; quiet discretion accompanies good sense.

It makes no sense to destroy someone else and slanderous words can do it quicker than a weapon. It's a total waist of God's most precious resource. Discretion that quietly takes care of business in a way that leaves other's lives in tack is not only kind, it's smart. Preserving human resources is always good business.

My Reflections and Responses:

_____

_____

_____

_____

_____

_____

_____

_____

_____

_____

_____

Date: _____   190

Proverbs 11:13 *A gadabout gossip can't be trusted with a secret, but someone of integrity won't violate a confidence.*

D on't share a secret with a gossip and ask them to keep it quiet. It's not in their nature and it's not in your best interest. Confide in a person of integrity and they will use your information to comfort and support you, not entertain their friends.

My Reflections and Responses:

_____

_____

_____

_____

_____

_____

_____

_____

_____

_____

_____

_____

Date: _____   191

Proverbs 11:14 *without good direction, people lose their way; the more wise counsel you follow, the better your chances.*

I f you're planning a trip to a place you've never been, ask directions from someone who knows the way. Better yet, ask several people who have been there. Each one might contribute a valuable piece of information that the others weren't aware of. It will make your trip a lot more enjoyable and you won't get lost.

My Reflections and Responses:

_____

_____

_____

_____

_____

_____

_____

_____

_____

_____

Date: _____   192

Proverbs 11:17 *When you're kind to others, you help yourself; when you're cruel to others, you hurt yourself.*

I f you were kind or cruel to another, that would indicate a single action. While it might be significant, a single act doesn't establish a pattern. Being kind or cruel to others is plural, indicating something you do many times. Your actions, repeated enough times, become your habit, tendency or inclination; in other words, it becomes a reflection of who you are. Ultimately, what you do to others, you're doing to yourself.

My Reflections and Responses:

_____

_____

_____

_____

_____

_____

_____

_____

_____

_____

Date: _____   193

Proverbs 11:22 *Like a gold ring in a pig's snout is a beautiful face on an empty head.*

A ring is actually only a symbol. Although beautiful to look at, its real value is in what it represents; marriage, love, friendship, or even a reflection of its wearer. That's why a gold ring in a pig's snout is such a waste; it has no real meaning so it has no value. A person's outward beauty is only worth what it's attached to.

My Reflections and Responses:

_____

_____

_____

_____

_____

_____

_____

_____

_____

_____

_____

Date: _____   194

Proverbs 11:24 *The world of the generous gets larger and larger; the world of the stingy gets smaller and smaller.*

A stingy person usually accumulates more and more stuff. How can their world get smaller and smaller when their pile of stuff gets larger and larger? Because the size of a person's world has nothing to do with stuff and everything to do with people; the size of a person's world is measured by the size of their heart.

My Reflections and Responses:

_____

_____

_____

_____

_____

_____

_____

_____

_____

_____

_____

Date: _____

Proverbs 11:27 *The one who seeks good finds delight; the student of evil becomes evil.*

The food we feed ourselves literally becomes a part of us. Good food produces pleasant results and vice versa. The information we feed ourselves, the knowledge we accumulate, affects our minds in much the same way. We don't notice the effect right away any more than we notice the benefit of broccoli the moment we eat it, but it begins to affect how we think and eventually who we are. We need to be aware of evil, but, if even only out of curiosity, we begin to delve into it too deeply, we risk an unintended result. No one intends to get fat on junk food, but eat enough of it and before you know it, you're there.

My Reflections and Responses:

_____

_____

_____

_____

_____

_____

_____

_____

Date: _____   196

Proverbs 11:28 *A life devoted to things is a dead life, a stump; a God-shaped life is a flourishing tree.*

Ve say something is dead when it has no life in it. Things aren't alive, and you can only get from anything, what it has to give. God is not only alive but he is life; if you want life, go to the one who has it to give.

My Reflections and Responses:

_____

_____

_____

_____

_____

_____

_____

_____

_____

_____

_____

_____

Date: _____   197

Proverbs 11:29 *Exploit or abuse your family, and end up with a fistful of air; common sense tells you it's a stupid way to live.*

Your family is an opportunity not a right. If you inherit the family business and don't take care of it, work it and protect it, before long you will end up destroying it, your inheritance worthless. Next to your relationship with God, family is your most important business and your greatest inheritance. If you neglect it, exploit it or abuse it, you will destroy it and end up with nothing. Love, accept, nurture and protect it, and your family, like a thriving business, will be an ongoing joy and resource to you, your children, your grandchildren and future generations.

My Reflections and Responses:

_____

_____

_____

_____

_____

_____

_____

_____

Date: _____   198

Proverbs 11:30 *A good life is a fruit-bearing tree; a violent life destroys souls.*

E veryone on this earth was created and intended to be productive. A good life is a productive one, fulfilling that destiny and enriching the lives of many. A violent life is far worse than an unproductive one. It not only robs the world of its own intended destiny, but also the destiny of others, who would have, in turn, enriched the lives of many others. The damage goes on and on, multiplying with each generation. Thank God, the good that one life can do has that same multiplying effect.

My Reflections and Responses:

_____

_____

_____

_____

_____

_____

_____

_____

_____

Date: _____

Proverbs 11:31 *If good people barely make it, what's in store for the bad!*

D on't be discouraged if you barely made it, thank God you made it! If you happen to have anything left over, don't waist it, give it away and help someone else make it. It's a tough world out there and everyone could use a little help. No one makes it on their own, and being bad certainly doesn't inspire anyone to lend a helping hand.

My Reflections and Responses:

_____

_____

_____

_____

_____

_____

_____

_____

_____

_____

_____

Date: _____   200

Proverbs 12:1 *If you love learning, you love the discipline that goes with it — how shortsighted to refuse correction!*

L earning and discipline are a package deal. If you'd love to have a new car but don't want to pay for it, I guess you don't really want it that much after all. If you're not willing to pay the price for what you want, it will always remain a wish and never become a reality.

My Reflections and Responses:

_____

_____

_____

_____

_____

_____

_____

_____

_____

_____

_____

Date: _____

Proverbs 12:4 A hearty wife invigorates her husband, but a frigid woman is cancer in the bones.

A hearty wife has something worth giving and when she gives it to her husband, he is invigorated. A frigid wife is lacking something, warmth; she can't give her husband something that she doesn't have so instead of invigorating him, she depletes him. Of course, the same can be said of a hearty husband.

My Reflections and Responses:

_____

_____

_____

_____

_____

_____

_____

_____

_____

_____

_____

Date: _____   202

Proverbs 12:10 *Good people are good to their animals; the "good-hearted" bad people kick and abuse them.*

No matter how good you treat your animal, he will never brag on you and tell others what a great person you are. How you treat him is an indication of who you really are when no one's looking. A "good-hearted" bad person is only "good" for show; if there isn't anything in it for them, if they aren't likely to get credit for it, why bother?

My Reflections and Responses:

_____

_____

_____

_____

_____

_____

_____

_____

_____

_____

Date: _____   203

Proverbs 12:11 *The one who stays on the job has food on the table; the witless chase whims and fancies.*

The witless, clueless, or unintelligent can't see the relationship between working and having the money to buy food. Their desires will always remain dreams, never becoming realities. They will continue to think the person with plenty just got lucky. They won't notice how hard that person worked to get so lucky.

My Reflections and Responses:

_____

_____

_____

_____

_____

_____

_____

_____

_____

_____

_____

Date: _____   204

Proverbs 12:15 Fools are headstrong and do what they like; wise people take advice.

A fool thinks he's smart, always doing just what he wants, ignoring all consequences, chasing after his own selfish desires. He looks at the wise man that listens to others advice, tries to do what is right, considers the effect his actions will have on others and calls him the fool. The headstrong fool spends his entire life looking for a happiness he will never find; how smart it that?

My Reflections and Responses:

_____

_____

_____

_____

_____

_____

_____

_____

_____

_____

Date: _____

Proverbs 12:16 *Fools have short fuses and explode all too quickly; the prudent quietly shrug off insults.*

Whoever lights the fools fuse controls him. The shorter the fuse, the easer he is to control. The wise man has no fuse with which to be controlled. He understands that insults diminish the insulter, not the insulted, so he quietly goes on his way.

My Reflections and Responses:

_____

_____

_____

_____

_____

_____

_____

_____

_____

_____

_____

_____

_____

Date: _____

Proverbs 12:25 *Worry weighs us down; a cheerful word picks us up.*

Worry is living with the fear that something terrible that hasn't actually happened, is bound to happen, if we don't worry enough about it happening. If that makes any sense to you, you'd make a perfect worrier.

My Reflections and Responses:

_____

_____

_____

_____

_____

_____

_____

_____

_____

_____

_____

_____

Date: _____

Proverbs 13:1 *Intelligent children listen to their parents; foolish children do their own thing.*

Whaat makes children who listen to their parents intelligent is first, accepting that they don't already know everything there is to know, second, believing that someone else just might have something helpful to teach them, and third, realizing that their parents probably love them more, and want them to succeed more than anyone else on earth, and will try the hardest to give them good advice.

My Reflections and Responses:

_____

_____

_____

_____

_____

_____

_____

_____

_____

_____

Date: _____

Proverbs 13:3 *Careful words make for a careful life; careless talk may ruin everything.*

Words are powerful; they cast a vision and determine a person's direction. Careful, well thought-out words are a reflection of what's going on inside a person; so are careless ones.

My Reflections and Responses:

_____

_____

_____

_____

_____

_____

_____

_____

_____

_____

_____

_____

_____

Date: _____

Proverbs 13:10 *Arrogant know-it-alls stir up discord, but wise men and women listen to each other's counsel.*

You can't tell an arrogant know-it-all anything because they think they know everything. That's just another way of saying they're better than everyone else; not a very good way of spreading peace and harmony. When wise men and women listen to each other's counsel, they're not only getting information but also giving validation. They might or might not find the information useful, but the good will that is generated by listening, and the opportunity to find out what others are thinking, are always invaluable.

My Reflections and Responses:

_____

_____

_____

_____

_____

_____

_____

_____

_____

Date: _____   210

Proverbs 13:12 *Unrelenting disappointment leaves you heartsick, but a sudden good break can turn life around.*

When you're heartsick, nothing else about you feels well. Discouragement is contagious. It starts in the heart, spreads to the mind and body, and before you know it, others around you start coming down with it. Encouragement can be just as contagious and one good break, at just the right time, can lift your spirits and give you the desire, energy and confidence to tackle what previously seemed insurmountable and over-whelming.

My Reflections and Responses:

_____

_____

_____

_____

_____

_____

_____

_____

_____

Date: _____

Proverbs 13:17 *Irresponsible talk makes a real mess of things, but a reliable reporter is a healing presence.*

I rresponsible talk cares nothing about accuracy or accountability, only about entertaining an audience, often at the expense of others. Someone who tells the truth in an accurate and compassionate way, offers more than information, he offers a chance for healing.

My Reflections and Responses:

_____

_____

_____

_____

_____

_____

_____

_____

_____

_____

_____

_____

Date: _____

Proverbs 13:20 *Become wise by walking with the wise; hang out with fools and watch your life fall to pieces.*

You will become one of the "people" you hang out with. First you tolerate, and then you accept, soon you get comfortable with, and eventually share their values and visions. It's called the process of desensitization, which means you'll get used to just about anything you expose yourself to long enough. Make sure you hang around the kind of people you want to become before you become the kind of person you don't want to be.

My Reflections and Responses:

_____

_____

_____

_____

_____

_____

_____

_____

_____

Date: _____   213

Proverbs 13:24 *A refusal to correct is a refusal to love; love your children by disciplining them.*

Letting your children go in the wrong direction without correcting them has nothing to do with loving them too much to discipline them. Either you're so afraid they might stop loving you that you can't risk upsetting them, or you just don't care enough about them to bother. Either way, it's all about you not them. Love your children enough to discipline them.

My Reflections and Responses:

_____

_____

_____

_____

_____

_____

_____

_____

_____

_____

Date: _____   214

Proverbs 14:5 *A true witness never lies; a false witness makes a business of it.*

If someone lies 10% of the time, you don't call them 90% truthful; you call them a liar. Even though they tell the truth most of the time, you never know when you can trust them, so you don't.

My Reflections and Responses:

_____

_____

_____

_____

_____

_____

_____

_____

_____

_____

_____

_____

_____

Date: _____   215

Proverbs 14:7 *Escape quickly from the company of fools; they're a waste of your time, a waste of your words.*

Don't avoid fools completely, you never know when circumstances might have made them ready to listen to reason, but as soon as you've determined it's a waste of time, save your breath, you've got better things to do.

My Reflections and Responses:

_____

_____

_____

_____

_____

_____

_____

_____

_____

_____

_____

Date: _____   216

Proverbs 14:12 *There's a way of life that looks harmless enough; look again — it leads straight to hell.*

Murder, rape and robbery never look harmless; good people have an easy enough time avoiding such things. It's a careless, lazy, selfish way of life that you have to look out for; it doesn't seem so bad, and it might take a little longer, but if you're not careful, you'll end up the same place all those murderers, rapists and robbers are headed.

My Reflections and Responses:

_____

_____

_____

_____

_____

_____

_____

_____

_____

_____

_____

Date: _____

Proverbs 14:14 *A mean person gets paid back in meanness, a gracious person in grace.*

Although not right, it's a lot easier to be mean to someone who's being mean than to someone who's being nice. Don't be surprised if you get back the same treatment you give others. Try doing the harder, not just the easer thing; be gracious to the next mean person you run in to. It might change their attitude but it will certainly change yours.

My Reflections and Responses:

_____

_____

_____

_____

_____

_____

_____

_____

_____

_____

_____

Date: _____

Proverbs 14:15 *The gullible believe anything they're told; the prudent sift and weigh every word.*

Being cautious and sensible doesn't make a person paranoid, just wise. The person who accepts everything as truth, is only helpful to those who would like to take advantage of them; no one else can rely on their judgment.

My Reflections and Responses:

_____

_____

_____

_____

_____

_____

_____

_____

_____

_____

_____

_____

Date: _____

Proverbs 14:17 *The hotheaded do things they'll later regret;*
the coldhearted get the cold shoulder.

The hotheaded are entirely emotion driven and
end up creating trouble for themselves. The
coldhearted are devoid of emotion and
behave in ways that result in rejection. The wise
feel and express emotions but are not controlled by
them and enjoy warm, healthy relationships.

My Reflections and Responses:

_____

_____

_____

_____

_____

_____

_____

_____

_____

_____

_____

Date: _____   220

Proverbs 14:18 *Foolish dreamers live in a world of illusion; wise realists plant their feet on the ground.*

In a dream, it never rains on their picnic, so the foolish person never comes prepared with an umbrella. The wise person, living in reality, comes prepared for sunshine or rain. A little adversity doesn't take them by surprise, so they are able to enjoy the picnic in less than ideal circumstances.

My Reflections and Responses:

_____

_____

_____

_____

_____

_____

_____

_____

_____

_____

_____

Date: _____   221

Proverbs 14:24 *The wise accumulate wisdom; fools get stupider by the day.*

I t just stands to reason that you'll get more and more of what you look for, collect, and surround yourself with. How many wise people have you ever seen searching for foolishness or vice versa? What you look hard enough for, you'll usually find.

My Reflections and Responses:

_____

_____

_____

_____

_____

_____

_____

_____

_____

_____

_____

_____

Date: _____

Proverbs 14:28 *The mark of a good leader is loyal followers; leadership is nothing without a following.*

If you're looking for a good leader, check out the quality of his followers; if they are fools, keep looking. He won't be a leader for long if he can't inspire intelligent followers.

My Reflections and Responses:

_____

_____

_____

_____

_____

_____

_____

_____

_____

_____

_____

_____

_____

_____

Date: _____   223

Proverbs 14:29 *Slowness to anger makes for deep understanding; a quick-tempered person stockpiles stupidity.*

W hen you get angry, you stop listening; how can you understand anything if you aren't listening? The quicker you get angry, the quicker you stop listening to anything except your own out of control, paranoid, self-centered self-talk. That's how you end up stockpiling stupidity.

My Reflections and Responses:

_____

_____

_____

_____

_____

_____

_____

_____

_____

_____

_____

Date: _____   224

Proverbs 14:30 *A sound mind makes for a robust body, but runaway emotions corrode the bones.*

A sound mind makes sound decisions about mind and body. An emotional wreck ends up falling apart in every way. A sound mind is formed and nurtured by decision and discipline, not destiny.

My Reflections and Responses:

_____

_____

_____

_____

_____

_____

_____

_____

_____

_____

_____

_____

Date: _____

Proverbs 14:34 *God-devotion makes a country strong; God-avoidance leaves people weak.*

It's people that make a country strong or weak. Devotion to God produces unity, harmony, happiness, and a healthy, disciplined lifestyle. Avoiding God results in lost, unhappy, disorganized individuals who care little about anything except their own selfish desires.

My Reflections and Responses:

_____

_____

_____

_____

_____

_____

_____

_____

_____

_____

_____

_____

_____

Date: _____   226

Proverbs 15:1 *A gentle response defuses anger, but a sharp tongue kindles a temper-fire.*

If a conflict is a fire, a gentle response is like pouring water on that fire. It wouldn't make sense to try stopping the fire by pouring gasoline on it, but that's exactly what we're doing when we respond with a sharp tongue. Be a fire extinguisher, not a fire starter and learn to distinguish water words from gasoline words.

My Reflections and Responses:

_____

_____

_____

_____

_____

_____

_____

_____

_____

_____

Date: _____

Proverbs 15:2 *Knowledge flows like spring water from the wise; fools are leaky faucets, dripping nonsense.*

Whatever fills a vessel is the only thing that can come out of it. If your vessel is full of wisdom, you'll want to deliberately pour it out on others. If it's full of nonsense, you'll probably want to hide it, but it's going to leak out anyway. Whatever you hold inside will eventually make its way out, either accidently or on purpose.

My Reflections and Responses:

_____

_____

_____

_____

_____

_____

_____

_____

_____

_____

_____

Date: _____

Proverbs 15:4 *Kind words heal and help; cutting words wound and maim.*

I f kind words heal and help, then there's already a wound that needs healing and helping. Whether you inflicted the wound or not, you can still be a healer with your words. If you approach the wounded with a knife, how is that going to help the healing? They will end up more deeply wounded, and you will have taken advantage of the weak. You won't be able to escape responsibility by claiming that you did it in self-defense, or for their own good.

My Reflections and Responses:

_____

_____

_____

_____

_____

_____

_____

_____

_____

Date: _____   229

Proverbs 15:12 *Know-it-alls don't like being told what to do; they avoid the company of wise men and women.*

If you're trying to sell a phony or a fake, never let the buyer see it up next to the real thing. They'll spot the forgery right away. That's probably why know-it-alls don't like to hang around wise men and women who actually know something.

My Reflections and Responses:

_____

_____

_____

_____

_____

_____

_____

_____

_____

_____

_____

Date: _____

Proverbs 15:13 *A cheerful heart brings a smile to your face; a sad heart makes it hard to get through the day.*

Your mood will color your face and your day. If others keep asking what's wrong before you say a word, your mood is probably showing through. You can't always be happy and smiley; sometimes really sad things happen in your life. If you share your feelings with someone who cared enough to notice and ask, they might just help you through your sad time and bring a smile back to your face.

My Reflections and Responses:

_____

_____

_____

_____

_____

_____

_____

_____

_____

_____

Date: _____   231

Proverbs 15:14 *An intelligent person is always eager to take in more truth; fools feed on fast-food fads and fancies.*

Truth is like a good steak. It takes some time and effort to chew it up and digest it, but you end up with something nutritious. Fads and fancies are like cotton candy; it takes no effort at all to consume, but you end up with nothing except maybe a tooth ache. A person's choices will tell you a lot about their intelligence.

My Reflections and Responses:

_____

_____

_____

_____

_____

_____

_____

_____

_____

_____

_____

Date: _____

Proverbs 15:18 *Hot tempers start fights; a calm, cool spirit keeps the peace.*

It's not the offensive or hurtful thing that someone says or does to you that starts a fight or keeps the peace. It's your response that determines the ultimate outcome. Your calm, cool actions put you in charge of the situation. Your hot tempered reaction gives the other person control. You are meant to lead, not follow.

My Reflections and Responses:

_____

_____

_____

_____

_____

_____

_____

_____

_____

_____

_____

Date: _____

Proverbs 15:22 *Refuse good advice and watch your plans fail; take good counsel and watch them succeed.*

I f you think you're the only one with a good idea, you probably won't waste your time listening to the advice of others. Listen to others and you'll benefit from their good ideas as well as your own. When you succeed, you can all celebrate.

My Reflections and Responses:

_____

_____

_____

_____

_____

_____

_____

_____

_____

_____

_____

_____

Proverbs 15:23 *Congenial conversation — what a pleasure!*
The right word at the right time — beautiful!

If you'd like for others to look forward to talking to you, work on your communication skills. Good communication is more than just accurate information. The right word at just the right time will be received by an appreciative audience.

My Reflections and Responses:

_____

_____

_____

_____

_____

_____

_____

_____

_____

_____

_____

_____

_____

Date: _____   235

Proverbs 16:6 *Guilt is banished through love and truth; Fear-of-GOD deflects evil.*

If you're guilty, with love and truth, confess your fault, make it right if you can, and forgive yourself. If someone else is guilty, with love and truth, forgive, and if they're willing, reconcile. Either way, love and truth have freed you from guilt through forgiveness.

My Reflections and Responses:

_____

_____

_____

_____

_____

_____

_____

_____

_____

_____

_____

_____

Date: _____   236

Proverbs 16:10 *A good leader motivates, doesn't mislead, doesn't exploit.*

A good leader serves his followers, he doesn't use them. His authority is conferred upon him by those willing to follow his wise leadership, not by dominating and controlling them. A tyrant will end up with only a few disloyal followers just waiting for the first sign of weakness so they can take over.

My Reflections and Responses:

_____

_____

_____

_____

_____

_____

_____

_____

_____

_____

_____

Date: _____

Proverbs 16:16 *Get wisdom — it's worth more than money; choose insight over income every time.*

Money is only a tool; you can't eat it, wear it, live in it or drive it. In the hands of a wise person, it can be used to accomplish much. It doesn't matter how much money an unwise person has, they will misuse it and end up with no money, and nothing accomplished with their original funds.

My Reflections and Responses:

_____

_____

_____

_____

_____

_____

_____

_____

_____

_____

_____

Date: _____   238

Proverbs 16:18 *First pride, then the crash — the bigger the ego, the harder the fall.*

The proud mistakenly believe they are their own god. When they try to stand on their own creation, it all comes crashing down and they soon discover that apart from the Creator of all things, they can accomplish nothing to be proud of.

My Reflections and Responses:

_____

_____

_____

_____

_____

_____

_____

_____

_____

_____

_____

_____

_____

Date: _____   239

Proverbs 16:25 *There's a way that looks harmless enough; look again — it leads straight to hell.*

When have you ever heard of a harmless person accomplishing anything noteworthy? They cause no trouble because they take no chances. Be a dangerous person, a risk taker, someone who's willing to fight and die for what they believe in. If you stand up for what's good, true and right, your reputation will be anything but harmless among the bad, dishonest and wrong in this world.

My Reflections and Responses:

_____

_____

_____

_____

_____

_____

_____

_____

_____

_____

Date: _____   240

Proverbs 17:8 *Receiving a gift is like getting a rare gemstone;*
any way you look at it, you see beauty refracted.

It's being given a gift that is the rare gemstone, not the gift itself. The beauty is in someone caring about you enough to give you something that is unearned, but in the eyes of the giver, well deserved.

My Reflections and Responses:

_____

_____

_____

_____

_____

_____

_____

_____

_____

_____

_____

_____

Date: _____

Proverbs 17:9 *Overlook an offense and bond a friendship; fasten on to a slight and — good-bye, friend!*

Would you rather have a friend or an enemy? Hang around anyone long enough and they're bound to offend you, if even unintentionally. Hang around that person long enough and you'll probably offend them as well. You can both forgive and get on with the friendship, or forget the whole thing and look for someone you can get along with perfectly, all the time; good luck finding that person.

My Reflections and Responses:

_____

_____

_____

_____

_____

_____

_____

_____

_____

_____

Proverbs 17:10 *A quiet rebuke to a person of good sense does more than a whack on the head of a fool.*

An intelligent person isn't someone who knows it all, but someone who can accept gentle criticism and become wiser for it. If they have to be hit up-side the head to get it, they're not that intelligent, they won't get it anyway, and you've just wasted your time and embarrassed yourself for being so harsh.

My Reflections and Responses:

_____

_____

_____

_____

_____

_____

_____

_____

_____

_____

_____

Date: _____   243

Proverbs 17:14 *The start of a quarrel is like a leak in a dam, so stop it before it bursts.*

A quarrel is just a disagreement. Stop it quickly and you'll probably forget all about it by tomorrow. Allow it to continue and a quarrel can turn into a war. Wars destroy lives on both sides of the conflict.

My Reflections and Responses:

_____

_____

_____

_____

_____

_____

_____

_____

_____

_____

_____

Date: _____

Proverbs 17:17 *Friends love through all kinds of weather, and families stick together in all kinds of trouble.*

A fair-weather friend is only there when things are going good; what kind of friend is that? A fowl weather friend is only there when you need rescuing; not that much better. A friend is a friend no matter what. Family is a lot like a friend only you don't get a choice.

My Reflections and Responses:

_____

_____

_____

_____

_____

_____

_____

_____

_____

_____

_____

_____

Date: _____

Proverbs 17:20 *A bad motive can't achieve a good end;*
double-talk brings you double trouble.

A poisoned tree doesn't produce good fruit
and bad, only poisoned fruit. You can't talk
your way out of responsibility for your own
bad acts, for your own selfish reasons, just because
some good might have come out of it. You know
that any good was by the grace of God, not by your
design or intent.

My Reflections and Responses:

_____

_____

_____

_____

_____

_____

_____

_____

_____

_____

Date: _____   246

Proverbs 17:22 *A cheerful disposition is good for your health; gloom and doom leave you bone-tired.*

Whatever your physical condition is, a cheerful attitude will improve it and a bad attitude will make it feel worse than it really is and might actually make it worse. Because they are always seeking balance or homeostasis, your mental attitude will bring your physical body right along with it.

My Reflections and Responses:

_____

_____

_____

_____

_____

_____

_____

_____

_____

_____

_____

_____

Date: _____

247

Proverbs 17:27 *The one who knows much says little; an understanding person remains calm.*

An understanding person isn't compelled to prove them self to others. They quietly contain their wisdom until it comes time to share it for the benefit of others, not to enhance their own status.

My Reflections and Responses:

_____

_____

_____

_____

_____

_____

_____

_____

_____

_____

_____

_____

Date: _____

Proverbs 17:28 *Even dunces who keep quiet are thought to be wise; as long as they keep their mouths shut, they're smart.*

I f he opens his mouth, a dunce proves his own stupidity. He will inevitably talk about a subject he knows nothing about, since he knows nothing about practically everything. If he just keeps quiet, others might give him the benefit of the doubt and assume he knows more than he really does. If you're stupid, at least be smart about it. Stupidity doesn't have to be a permanent condition; it can be cured by quietly acquiring knowledge from someone who really knows something.

My Reflections and Responses:

_____

_____

_____

_____

_____

_____

_____

_____

_____

Date: _____   249

Proverbs 18:6 *The words of a fool start fights; do him a favor and gag him.*

A fool doesn't know the meaning of the word diplomacy. He's like an arsonist, starting fires everywhere he goes. Deny him the opportunity to stir things up with his inflammatory prattle and you will be doing everyone a favor.

My Reflections and Responses:

_____

_____

_____

_____

_____

_____

_____

_____

_____

_____

_____

_____

Date: _____   250

Proverbs 18:7 *Fools are undone by their big mouths; their souls are crushed by their words.*

I f they would just keep quiet, their ignorance wouldn't hurt themselves or others, but they just can't stop themselves; if they could, they wouldn't be fools. Imagine how much force it takes to crush something, that's how much destructive power fools words have.

My Reflections and Responses:

_____

_____

_____

_____

_____

_____

_____

_____

_____

_____

_____

Date: _____

Proverbs 18:8 *Listening to gossip is like eating cheap candy; do you really want junk like that in your belly?*

Candy has empty calories; it fills you up with something of no nutritional value and takes away your desire for something that might actually be of benefit. Candy isn't real food and gossip isn't real information; they're both just cheap imitations.

My Reflections and Responses:

_____

_____

_____

_____

_____

_____

_____

_____

_____

_____

_____

_____

Date: _____   252

Proverbs 18:13 *Answering before listening is both stupid and rude.*

H ow can you respond wisely to something you haven't even heard? You'll just be telling someone what you want them to know, not what they need to know.

My Reflections and Responses:

_____

_____

_____

_____

_____

_____

_____

_____

_____

_____

_____

_____

_____

Date: _____

Proverbs 18:17 *The first speech in a court case is always convincing — until the cross-examination starts!*

Never think you know the real story by listening to only one side. Both parties could be telling the truth but giving two entirely different stories, because each sees it from only their own perspective. Information is always colored by motivation and interpretation.

My Reflections and Responses:

_____

_____

_____

_____

_____

_____

_____

_____

_____

_____

_____

_____

Date: _____   254

Proverbs 18:21 *Words kill, words give life; they're either poison or fruit — you choose.*

God's Word created everything; that's how powerful words are. Choose your words as carefully as you would point a loaded gun. You wouldn't carelessly discharge a weapon into a crowd and expect to escape responsibility when someone accidently got hurt would you? Be just as prepared to accept responsibility for the healing or hurt your words cause.

My Reflections and Responses:

_____

_____

_____

_____

_____

_____

_____

_____

_____

_____

_____

Date: _____   255

Proverbs 18:22 *Find a good spouse, you find a good life —*
and even more: the favor of GOD!

B ecause in marriage, two become one, you can't have a good life apart from your spouse and they can't have one apart from you. God instituted marriage as a favor to his children, and to give them a little glimpse of the ecstasies they will one day share with him in heaven. If marriage turns into a living hell, it's certainly not because God designed it that way.

My Reflections and Responses:

_____

_____

_____

_____

_____

_____

_____

_____

_____

_____

_____

_____

Date: _____

Proverbs 19:3 *People ruin their lives by their own stupidity, so why does GOD always get blamed?*

If someone exercises their free will and insists on jumping off of a cliff, half way to the bottom isn't the best time to turn their life over to God and hope for a different result. He created them all right, and will save their sole, but in all likelihood, their body will obey God's, not Newton's law of gravity.

My Reflections and Responses:

_____

_____

_____

_____

_____

_____

_____

_____

_____

_____

_____

Date: _____   257

Proverbs 19:11 *Smart people know how to hold their tongue; their grandeur is to forgive and forget.*

S mart people don't always hold their tongue, but they know how. Sometimes speaking up is the right thing to do, and they don't hesitate, but sometimes keeping quiet serves a greater, and more loving good, and they know the difference. Intelligent people want to impact their future and know that can only be accomplished by living in the present, not by holding on to past grievances where change never occurs. Their ability to forgive, forget, and get on with life is a magnificent thing.

My Reflections and Responses:

_____

_____

_____

_____

_____

_____

_____

_____

_____

Date: _____   258

Proverbs 19:13 *A parent is worn to a frazzle by a stupid child; a nagging spouse is a leaky faucet.*

Family can be your greatest joy or biggest challenge. If you have a stupid child, before you give up on them out of frustration, remember where they didn't learn everything they didn't learn. You might need to learn a few things about parenting before you're able to teach them a thing or two about life. Don't be a nagging spouse. Your spouse will never be thirsty for what you have to say, even when it's important, because it continually comes out in dribbles and drabs. Give them a chance to look forward to what you have to say. If you're married to a nag, remember that they are still your gift from God; you might need to help them stop the leak before you can fully appreciate the blessing.

My Reflections and Responses:

_____

_____

_____

_____

_____

_____

Date: _____

Proverbs 19:18 *Discipline your children while you still have the chance; indulging them destroys them.*

You have a limited number of years to discipline your children and in doing so, help set a course for their lives. A lack of discipline won't destroy them while they are still with you; it's later on in their lives, when you are no longer there to protect them that your failure becomes their failed future. They won't know how to exercise the self-control necessary to succeed when life gets hard.

My Reflections and Responses:

_____

_____

_____

_____

_____

_____

_____

_____

_____

_____

Date: _____

Proverbs 19:19 *Let angry people endure the backlash of their own anger; if you try to make it better, you'll only make it worse.*

If you don't let angry people suffer the consequences of their own bad temper, you might be removing the very tool that God is using to teach them a better way; it's called enabling and eventually makes things worse for them and you.

My Reflections and Responses:

_____

_____

_____

_____

_____

_____

_____

_____

_____

_____

_____

_____

Date: _____   261

Proverbs 19:20 *Take good counsel and accept correction —*
that's the way to live wisely and well.

To insure their counsel is good, you need to surround yourself with good, wise people of God. When they correct you, accept it as a blessing and a gift from God. You will be adding their wisdom to your own, and have a much better life because of it.

My Reflections and Responses:

_____

_____

_____

_____

_____

_____

_____

_____

_____

_____

_____

Date: _____

Proverbs 20:1 *Wine makes you mean, beer makes you quarrelsome — a staggering drunk is not much fun.*

Although you won't be aware of it until the next morning, being intoxicated only creates trouble, it never avoids it. When you reach the point of staggering, you've long since left all reason and moderation behind. You're likely to have more than one mess to clean up after it's all over.

My Reflections and Responses:

_____

_____

_____

_____

_____

_____

_____

_____

_____

_____

_____

Date: _____   263

Proverbs 20:3 *It's a mark of good character to avert quarrels, but fools love to pick fights.*

The person who enjoys fighting, gets a kick out of destroying things; whether they're breaking furniture, friendships, or bones, it's not a very smart way to live. A person with a good heart would rather avoid a fight and show their strength of character than their power to bully and control others. Real strength is expressed by controlling your own impulses and temper.

My Reflections and Responses:

_____

_____

_____

_____

_____

_____

_____

_____

_____

_____

Date: _____   264

Proverbs 20:11 *Young people eventually reveal by their actions if their motives are on the up and up.*

L isten to what they say, but believe what you see. Their actions will eventually expose their hearts, whether good or bad. Don't be too critical of one or two missteps, remember, they're young and just learning, but before long you'll see a pattern of behavior that will show you the truth.

My Reflections and Responses:

_____

_____

_____

_____

_____

_____

_____

_____

_____

_____

_____

Date: _____   265

Proverbs 20:18 *Form your purpose by asking for counsel, then carry it out using all the help you can get.*

D on't go off all on your own, thinking that you need no advice or help from others. If anyone could have been self-sufficient, it would have been Jesus, but even he gathered disciples and many others close to him. If every life is a puzzle, God will personally give each of us many of the peaces needed to form our own picture, but there will always be missing pieces that we can only get from others, and others can only get from us. God's design ensures co-operation and participation among his children for each to complete their own picture and fulfill their own destiny; it's called the family of God for a reason.

My Reflections and Responses:

_____

_____

_____

_____

_____

_____

_____

_____

Date: _____ 266

Proverbs 20:19 *Gossips can't keep secrets, so never confide in blabbermouths.*

Gossips wouldn't keep secrets if they could, but they can't, so don't expect them to. It's their life blood; an anemic attempt at getting attention, sounding important, and entertaining themselves and others at the expense of anyone. On the other hand, if you want everyone to know something, tell a gossip and ask them to keep it quiet.

My Reflections and Responses:

_____

_____

_____

_____

_____

_____

_____

_____

_____

_____

_____

Date: _____   267

Proverbs 21:9 *Better to live alone in a tumbledown shack than share a mansion with a nagging spouse.*

Even though you'd rather live alone than with a nagging spouse, God didn't give you that option; you obviously have a lot of relationship work to do so you might as well get started as soon as possible. Keeping your promises to your spouse might be a good place to start and could eliminate much of the nagging.

My Reflections and Responses:

_____

_____

_____

_____

_____

_____

_____

_____

_____

_____

_____

Date: _____   268

Proverbs 21:11 *Simpletons only learn the hard way, but the wise learn by listening.*

I f you can learn by listening, you can benefit from other's mistakes; you don't have to make all of them yourself. If you can only learn by experience, you will only have time to learn very few things in your lifetime because experience is an important but slow process. There are some things you will want to see and do for yourself, but you can explore the entire universe if you're willing to listen to others; it's the only real way to time travel.

My Reflections and Responses:

_____

_____

_____

_____

_____

_____

_____

_____

_____

_____

Date: _____

Proverbs 21:17 *You're addicted to thrills? What an empty life! The pursuit of pleasure is never satisfied.*

If you're searching for the ultimate thrill, you'll always be disappointed and forever searching, because it can never be found. The things that thrill you today won't thrill you tomorrow; you'll continue to need bigger, better, and more outrageous experiences because old thrills get old and quickly lose their ability to pump that adrenalin that you've become addicted to. Pursue a life of faith, hope and love and they won't get old or ware out; your life will just keep getting better and better.

My Reflections and Responses:

_____

_____

_____

_____

_____

_____

_____

_____

Date: _____

Proverbs 21:19 *Better to live in a tent in the wild than with a cross and petulant spouse.*

I f living in a tent in the wild isn't your kind of fun, think about working on your relationship. Ask yourself if you might be contributing to your spouse's bad attitude; if you are, work on your own attitude and actions. Even if you have nothing to do with their bad mood, remember, a good mood can be as contagious as a bad one; you might need to start a new trend and set a different tone in your home.

My Reflections and Responses:

_____

_____

_____

_____

_____

_____

_____

_____

_____

_____

Date: _____

Proverbs 21:23 *Watch your words and hold your tongue; you'll save yourself a lot of grief.*

B e careful what you say and how much you say. Honesty doesn't require you to say everything that's on your mind; just make sure what you do say is the truth, and doesn't leave a false impression. Don't tell a half truth which is using bits and pieces of the truth to tell a lie and isn't really the truth at all. Don't be a blabbermouth who tells all, offends all, and causes all kinds of trouble for themselves and others.

My Reflections and Responses:

_____

_____

_____

_____

_____

_____

_____

_____

_____

_____

Date: _____   272

Proverbs 21:26 *Sinners are always wanting what they don't have; the God-loyal are always giving what they do have.*

Of course sinners are always wanting what they don't have; greed and selfishness is what caused them to sin in the first place. God-loyal people have confidence that God will continually supply their needs so they can concentrate on other people and on giving away what they do have.

My Reflections and Responses:

_____

_____

_____

_____

_____

_____

_____

_____

_____

_____

_____

_____

Date: _____   273

Proverbs 21:31 *Do your best, prepare for the worst — then trust GOD to bring victory.*

Preparing for the worst isn't expecting the worst; that would be pessimistic. Trusting in God means believing that doing your best, with God's help, will get you through even the worst of times if they do happen to come along, and will ultimately result in victory.

My Reflections and Responses:

_____

_____

_____

_____

_____

_____

_____

_____

_____

_____

_____

_____

Date: _____   274

Proverbs 22:6 *Point your kids in the right direction — when they're old they won't be lost.*

Point your kids, don't drag, beat or bully them; it won't teach them what they need to know. Pointing means giving them good directions and letting them learn to live their own lives with your support and guidance. If you don't allow them to begin making some of their own decisions, even occasional bad ones, they'll never develop the confidence they'll need to eventually find their own way when you're no longer around to help.

My Reflections and Responses:

_____

_____

_____

_____

_____

_____

_____

_____

_____

_____

Date: _____

Proverbs 22:14 *The mouth of a whore is a bottomless pit; you'll fall in that pit if you're on the outs with GOD.*

A bottomless pit goes on forever; it can never be filled, fulfilled, or satisfied. If you're not in a real relationship with the only one who can fill and fulfill you, God, you'll fall for every cheep imitation relationship that comes along. You'll settle for meaningless sex instead of meaningful love, instant gratification rather than eternal satisfaction.

My Reflections and Responses:

_____

_____

_____

_____

_____

_____

_____

_____

_____

_____

_____

Date: _____   276

Proverbs 22:24-25 *22 Don't hang out with angry people; don't keep company with hotheads. 25 Bad temper is contagious — don't get infected.*

Haven't you heard the old saying, "you're known for the company you keep"? Where do you think that saying came from? Don't think you can hang around a group without becoming like that group. If you're hanging around a group, you already are a part of that group. If you weren't willing to accept and adopt their attitudes and actions, you wouldn't be hanging out with them. Bad temper is contagious but so is good temper; choose your infection wisely.

My Reflections and Responses:

_____

_____

_____

_____

_____

_____

_____

_____

_____

Date: _____

Proverbs 23:22 *Listen with respect to the father who raised you, and when your mother grows old, don't neglect her.*

You won't always agree with him, and you might not always take his advice, but you should always listen to your father with respect. There could even come a time when you don't respect what your father is doing, but there should never come a time when you stop treating him with respect. Respect is earned by the other person or not; treating someone with respect is a reflection of who you are inside and has little to do with the other person. When your mother grows old, she will need a little extra help and attention even when what she has to say isn't the most interesting thing you've ever heard. Hopefully, she will have earned it with the help and attention she gave you when you were young and helpless; if not, do it anyway as a gift to God who has certainly been there for you in your time of need.

My Reflections and Responses:

_____

_____

_____

_____

_____

Date: _____   278

Proverbs 23:29-35 *29 Who are the people who are always crying the blues? Who do you know who reeks of self-pity? Who keeps getting beat up for no reason at all? Whose eyes are bleary and bloodshot? 30 It's those who spend the night with a bottle, for whom drinking is serious business. 31 Don't judge wine by its label, or its bouquet, or its full-bodied flavor. 32 Judge it rather by the hangover it leaves you with —the splitting headache, the queasy stomach. 33 Do you really prefer seeing double, with your speech all slurred, 34 Reeling and seasick, drunk as a sailor? 35 "They hit me," you'll say, "but it didn't hurt; they beat on me, but I didn't feel a thing. When I'm sober enough to manage it, bring me another drink!"*

Addicts haven't changed a bit. They're a pitiful waist of a wonderful resource. Whether it's alcohol, drugs, gambling, sex, or the dozens of other things people get addicted to, don't be fooled by the momentary high; look at the toll it takes the next day, week, month and years of a person's life, if you can even call that living. The only thing an addict looks forward to is more of the very thing that is destroying them.

My Reflections and Responses:

_____

_____

_____

_____

Date: _____   279

Proverbs 24:10 *If you fall to pieces in a crisis, there wasn't much to you in the first place.*

What is the glue that holds you together? Does it work when you really need it? It not, try a different brand, something that sticks with you no matter what you're going through, never gets old or wears out, just keeps getting stronger and better and lasts a lifetime. Faith in Jesus is a lot like that, the only brand you can always depend on.

My Reflections and Responses:

_____

_____

_____

_____

_____

_____

_____

_____

_____

_____

_____

Date: _____   280

Proverbs 24:26 *An honest answer is like a warm hug.*

Y ou don't have to test it, try to figure it out or determine if it's real or not; you can just accept and enjoy it. It's really nice to give and receive that kind of hug.

My Reflections and Responses:

_____

_____

_____

_____

_____

_____

_____

_____

_____

_____

_____

_____

_____

Date: _____

Proverbs 25:8 *Don't jump to conclusions — there may be a perfectly good explanation for what you just saw.*

There are usually a dozen possible explanations for just about anything. Don't automatically accept the worst as the most likely to be true. What would it hurt to check it out; you might be pleasantly surprised. You'll be better prepared to act when you've taken the time to get accurate information, no matter what the real explanation turns out to be.

My Reflections and Responses:

_____

_____

_____

_____

_____

_____

_____

_____

_____

_____

Date: _____

Proverbs 25:15 *Patient persistence pierces through indifference; gentle speech breaks down rigid defenses.*

Apathy develops over a long period of time. An indifferent person is resistant to quick change because they have reached a point where they just don't care about anything. They believe that if you don't care, you can't be disappointed or hurt. You can't combat that kind of discouragement with a quick fix or a momentary effort. You have to be consistent, persistent, gentle, caring and most importantly, never give up.

My Reflections and Responses:

_____

_____

_____

_____

_____

_____

_____

_____

_____

_____

_____

Date: _____

Proverbs 25:20 *Singing light songs to the heavyhearted is like pouring salt in their wounds.*

Y ou wouldn't think of celebrating someone else's misfortune but being cheerful around them while they're going through a difficult time will feel like that. You don't have to be sad and gloomy, but be sensitive to those who are.

My Reflections and Responses:

_____

_____

_____

_____

_____

_____

_____

_____

_____

_____

_____

_____

Date: _____   284

Proverbs 25:21-22 *21 If you see your enemy hungry, go buy him lunch; if he's thirsty, bring him a drink. 22 Your generosity will surprise him with goodness, and GOD will look after you.*

Y ou are God's representative, especially around your enemies; your friends probably already know about God's love or you wouldn't have enough in common with them to be friends. How are your enemies going to know about God's incredible love and generosity if his representative doesn't show it to them? Don't worry about the risk; God's got you covered.

My Reflections and Responses:

_____

_____

_____

_____

_____

_____

_____

_____

_____

_____

Date: _____

Proverbs 25:26 A good person who gives in to a bad person is a muddied spring, a polluted well.

When a good person gives in to a bad person, they are no longer a good person. They don't have to agree with the bad person to be corrupted, just go along with them.

My Reflections and Responses:

_____

_____

_____

_____

_____

_____

_____

_____

_____

_____

_____

_____

Proverbs 25:28 *A person without self-control is like a house with its doors and windows knocked out.*

A person without self-control can't hold anything in or keep anything out; they have no barriers or boundaries in their life. Nothing is private, sacred, protected or rejected so nothing has real value to them.

My Reflections and Responses:

_____

_____

_____

_____

_____

_____

_____

_____

_____

_____

_____

_____

Date: _____

Proverbs 26:2 *You have as little to fear from an undeserved curse as from the dart of a wren or the swoop of a swallow.*

An undeserved curse has no power over you other than a momentary distraction or slight irritation. Now a deserved curse is another matter; it's not actually the curse you need to be concerned with, but your bad behavior that brought the curse on in the first place. That's something to pay attention to and correct.

My Reflections and Responses:

_____

_____

_____

_____

_____

_____

_____

_____

_____

_____

_____

Date: _____   288

Proverbs 26:7 *A proverb quoted by fools is limp as a wet noodle.*

Words can be tools or weapons and are powerful only in the hands of someone who understands and knows how to use them. A fool might use a gun as a hammer with disastrous results to himself and those around him.

My Reflections and Responses:

_____

_____

_____

_____

_____

_____

_____

_____

_____

_____

_____

_____

Date: _____   289

Proverbs 26:9 *To ask a moron to quote a proverb is like putting a scalpel in the hands of a drunk.*

A wise saying is only wise when used wisely. When have you ever seen a moron use anything wisely? Like a scalpel, a proverb cuts to the heart of the matter; a little too far to the left or right or just a little too deeply and it could slice right through the heart. Dispensing wisdom is a very delicate operation.

My Reflections and Responses:

_____

_____

_____

_____

_____

_____

_____

_____

_____

_____

_____

Date: _____

Proverbs 26:16 *Dreamers fantasize their self-importance; they think they are smarter than a whole college faculty.*

Because they live in a fantasy world, dreamers are always right. They are superheroes in their own minds. In the real world, they would actually have to perform, not just pretend, so they stick with their imagination, where it takes no real effort to succeed. The first thing a genuinely smart person learns is how little they really know.

My Reflections and Responses:

_____

_____

_____

_____

_____

_____

_____

_____

_____

_____

_____

Date: _____

Proverbs 26:17 *You grab a mad dog by the ears when you butt into a quarrel that's none of your business.*

When you grab a mad dog by the ears, you'll quickly realize that you need to let go but it's too late. Let go and be mauled or hang on and be consumed. The best thing to do is leave a mad dog alone.

My Reflections and Responses:

_____

_____

_____

_____

_____

_____

_____

_____

_____

_____

_____

_____

Date: _____   292

Proverbs 26:18-19   *18 People who shrug off deliberate deceptions, saying, "I didn't mean it, I was only joking," 19 are worse than careless campers who walk away from smoldering campfires.*

S aying "I didn't mean it" doesn't turn a deception into a joke; it's just a cowardly attempt at avoid responsibility for the lie after being caught. Those people couldn't care less about the effect their actions have on other people's lives.

My Reflections and Responses:

_____

_____

_____

_____

_____

_____

_____

_____

_____

_____

_____

Date: _____   293

Proverbs 26:20 *When you run out of wood, the fire goes out; when the gossip ends, the quarrel dies down.*

To end the quarrel, you don't actually have to do anything except refuse to participate. Eventually, it will die down for lack of fuel. If you'd like quicker results, pour water on the fire with a kind word.

My Reflections and Responses:

_____

_____

_____

_____

_____

_____

_____

_____

_____

_____

_____

_____

Date: _____   294

Proverbs 26:21 *A quarrelsome person in a dispute is like kerosene thrown on a fire.*

You can't drown out a fire no matter how much kerosene you throw on it. You can't settle a dispute no how much you argue. Try something else; listen to the other side and acknowledge their position even if you don't agree with their conclusion.

My Reflections and Responses:

_____

_____

_____

_____

_____

_____

_____

_____

_____

_____

_____

_____

Date: _____   295

Proverbs 27:4 *We're blasted by anger and swamped by rage, but who can survive jealousy?*

As powerful and devastating as anger and rage can be, jealousy is the nuclear option when it comes to destructive emotions. It can destroy the jealous person, the object of their jealousy, and anyone else who happens to get in the way. Jealousy is not love, doesn't resemble love, and has none of the characteristics of love. It cares only for itself, hates anyone who gets in its way and is never satisfied or appeased.

My Reflections and Responses:

_____

_____

_____

_____

_____

_____

_____

_____

_____

_____

_____

Date: _____

Proverbs 27:5 *A spoken reprimand is better than approval that's never expressed.*

Y   ou can get to know someone who tells you
    how they feel; even if you don't like what
    they say, you'll know where you stand. The
person who doesn't communicate with you might as
well hate you as love you for all the good it does
you. They will remain a stranger, unknown and
untrusted.

My Reflections and Responses:

_____

_____

_____

_____

_____

_____

_____

_____

_____

_____

_____

Date: _____   297

Proverbs 27:15-16 *15 A nagging spouse is like the drip, drip, drip of a leaky faucet; 16 You can't turn it off, and you can't get away from it.*

It's not the drip that drives you crazy, it's the constant drip. Make sure you've listened the first time so it doesn't have to be repeated over and over. After you've listened and responded appropriately, you've done your part; let the rest go and don't drip back.

My Reflections and Responses:

_____

_____

_____

_____

_____

_____

_____

_____

_____

_____

Date: _____   298

Proverbs 27:21 *The purity of silver and gold is tested by putting them in the fire; the purity of human hearts is tested by giving them a little fame.*

When gold and silver is exposed to the fire, all the impurities are burned away and what remains is the real thing. When the human heart is exposed to a little fame, all pretenses are exposed and what you end up with is the real thing, good or bad. If you feel superior to those who lift you up, you'll exploit them. If you're humbled by the honor, you'll show your gratitude.

My Reflections and Responses:

_____

_____

_____

_____

_____

_____

_____

_____

_____

_____

Date: _____

Proverbs 28:2 *When the country is in chaos, everybody has a plan to fix it — But it takes a leader of real understanding to straighten things out.*

By the time the country reaches the point of chaos, everyone has had his say and nothing has worked. It's obvious that common sense isn't enough to save the day. It will take an uncommon leader, relying on an infallible source, to take the country in as yet an unimagined direction. Could anyone except a mighty man or woman of God fit that bill?

My Reflections and Responses:

_____

_____

_____

_____

_____

_____

_____

_____

_____

Date: _____   300

Proverbs 28:7 *Practice God's law — get a reputation for wisdom; hang out with a loose crowd — embarrass your family.*

Practicing God's law is wise, whether you have great understanding or not. Find the smartest person you know, do what they do, and you'll get a reputation for being as smart as they are. Hang out with stupid people and you will get a reputation that will embarrass you and your family.

My Reflections and Responses:

_____

_____

_____

_____

_____

_____

_____

_____

_____

_____

_____

Date: _____

Proverbs 28:9 *God has no use for the prayers of the people who won't listen to him.*

Have you ever had a conversation with a person who stuck both fingers in their ears every time you responded? Why would God talk to someone with their fingers in their ears, even if they'd just asked for directions? It would be a waste of his time and theirs.

My Reflections and Responses:

_____

_____

_____

_____

_____

_____

_____

_____

_____

_____

_____

_____

Date: _____   302

Proverbs 28:21 *Playing favorites is always a bad thing; you can do great harm in seemingly harmless ways.*

Showing someone favor can be a generous act; a loving, unearned gesture expressed out of the goodness of your heart. Playing favorites is a hurtful act; arbitrarily extending favor to one person and withholding it from another. It's not the extending but the withholding for no good reason that causes the problem. It sets up an artificial merit system based on nothing but a momentary whim or a selfish attempt to manipulate.

My Reflections and Responses:

_____

_____

_____

_____

_____

_____

_____

_____

_____

_____

Date: _____

Proverbs 29:15 *Wise discipline imparts wisdom; spoiled adolescents embarrass their parents*

Wise discipline takes many things into consideration and is given in a firm but loving way; it imparts wisdom because it is based on logic, reason and genuine care for the person, not anger at them for not obeying. Wise discipline isn't punishment, its instruction and correction; not necessarily pleasant, but never harsh and unkind.

My Reflections and Responses:

_____

_____

_____

_____

_____

_____

_____

_____

_____

_____

_____

Date: _____   304

Proverbs 29:17 *Discipline your children; you'll be glad you did — they'll turn out delightful to live with.*

Delightful children aren't born, they are raised with care. Ignore them or overindulge them and you'll create a disaster in your own home. Do yourself and your future grandchildren a favor, discipline your children.

My Reflections and Responses:

_____

_____

_____

_____

_____

_____

_____

_____

_____

_____

_____

_____

Date: _____

Proverbs 29:20 *Observe the people who always talk before they think — even simpletons are better off than they are.*

Quiet simpletons might be thought to be smarter than they really are. If they think before they speak, they'll only talk about what they know, even if it isn't much. Speak before you think and you'll expose your ignorance to everyone within the sound of your voice.

My Reflections and Responses:

_____

_____

_____

_____

_____

_____

_____

_____

_____

_____

_____

_____

Date: _____   306

Proverbs 29:21 *If you let people treat you like a doormat,
you'll be quite forgotten in the end.*

No one notices the doormat; it's just a way of getting from the outside to the inside without tracking in the dirt on your feet. If you act like a doormat, all you'll get is other people's dirt, and they won't even notice that they've stepped all over you.

My Reflections and Responses:

_____

_____

_____

_____

_____

_____

_____

_____

_____

_____

_____

_____

_____

Date: _____   307

Proverbs 29:25 *The fear of human opinion disables; trusting in GOD protects you from that.*

Human opinion isn't based on the truth, only on what each individual thinks. If your goal is to please others, because each person has a different opinion, you'll never succeed. The impossibility of the task will immobilize you and you'll accomplish nothing. Trusting in God, who is forever true, never contradictory, and always there to empower you, is the only proven path to success.

My Reflections and Responses:

_____

_____

_____

_____

_____

_____

_____

_____

_____

_____

Date: _____

Proverbs 30:12 *Don't imagine yourself to be quite presentable when you haven't had a bath in weeks.*

It's easy to minimize or overlook completely, our own offenses. We can rationalize, justify, and simply ignore in ourselves, what we would find totally unacceptable in others. Take a good look at yourself and if you find that too difficult, ask for and accept feedback from someone you trust to give you an honest assessment of how you look, act, and yes, even smell.

My Reflections and Responses:

_____

_____

_____

_____

_____

_____

_____

_____

_____

_____

_____

_____

Date: _____

Proverbs 30:15 *A leech has twin daughters named "Gimme" and "Gimme more."*

Y ou can never satisfy someone who has attached themselves to you and is trying to live their life through you. They will suck you dry and come back for more. It's not in a dependent person's nature to contribute, only to take; if you know someone like that, or are someone like that, separate immediately so both of you can get a life of your own.

My Reflections and Responses:

_____

_____

_____

_____

_____

_____

_____

_____

_____

_____

_____

Date: _____

Proverbs 30:18 *Three things amaze me, no, four things I'll never understand*

There are some things that are simply beyond our ability to comprehend. Enjoy them, avoid them, or pray for the grace to get through them.

My Reflections and Responses:

_____

_____

_____

_____

_____

_____

_____

_____

_____

_____

_____

_____

_____

Date: _____   311

Proverbs 30:19 *how an eagle flies so high in the sky, how a snake glides over a rock, how a ship navigates the ocean, why adolescents act the way they do.*

No one will ever fully understand adolescents, not even themselves; no longer children, not yet adults, they have so much to figure out, they often get totally lost in an attempt to find their way. Be kind to them and as patient as possible, even though you don't understand. One day most of them will kind of get it and sort of grow up into mostly mature adults. When that happens, you might just long for the days when they were just kids.

My Reflections and Responses:

_____

_____

_____

_____

_____

_____

_____

_____

_____

Date: _____   312

Proverbs 30:21 *Three things are too much for even the earth to bear, yes, four things shake its foundations...*

O ccasionally things are so upside-down and backwards it's like a common sense earthquake; that's when you have to abandon reason and logic and just hold on to faith for dear life.

My Reflections and Responses:

_____

_____

_____

_____

_____

_____

_____

_____

_____

_____

_____

_____

_____

Date: _____   313

Proverbs 30:22 *When the janitor becomes the boss, when a fool gets rich.*

It's like winning the lottery; when someone suddenly acquires all that wealth without earning it or knowing what to do with it, they usually loose it within the year.

My Reflections and Responses:

_____

_____

_____

_____

_____

_____

_____

_____

_____

_____

_____

_____

Date: _____ 314

Proverbs 30:23 *When a whore is voted "woman of the year," when a "girlfriend" replaces a faithful wife.*

A prostitute isn't the epitome of womanhood; she's the pity of womanhood whose condition warrants intervention, not celebration. Being a "girlfriend" to another woman's husband is like being a fantasy wife; she doesn't have to clean the house, do the dishes, bare and raise the children or put up with her husband's selfishness. If the fantasy ever becomes reality, the husband and girlfriend are in for a big surprise because the only genuine person in the whole affair is the faithful wife.

My Reflections and Responses:

_____

_____

_____

_____

_____

_____

_____

_____

_____

Date: _____   315

Proverbs 30:32-33 *32 If you're dumb enough to call attention to yourself by offending people and making rude gestures, 33 don't be surprised if someone bloodies your nose. Churned milk turns into butter; riled emotions turn into fist fights.*

If you keep looking for a fight by picking on others, you'll eventually run into someone as immature as you, who will be glad to oblige you. If you happen to come across someone that dumb, be the mature one and ignore the insult; let them end up the one looking like a fool.

My Reflections and Responses:

_____

_____

_____

_____

_____

_____

_____

_____

_____

_____

_____

Date: _____   316

Proverbs 31:10, 16-31 *10 A good woman is hard to find, and worth far more than diamonds. 16 She looks over a field and buys it, then, with money she's put aside, plants a garden... 18 She senses the worth of her work, is in no hurry to call it quits for the day... 20 She's quick to assist anyone in need, reaches out to help the poor... 23 Her husband is greatly respected when he deliberates with the city fathers... she always faces tomorrow with a smile. 26 When she speaks she has something worthwhile to say, and she always says it kindly. 27 She keeps an eye on everyone in her household, and keeps them all busy and productive. 28 Her children respect and bless her; her husband joins in with words of praise: 29 "Many women have done wonderful things, but you've outclassed them all!" 30 Charm can mislead and beauty soon fades. The woman to be admired and praised is the woman who lives in the Fear-of-GOD. 31 Give her everything she deserves! Festoon her life with praises!*

A diamond doesn't nothing but look pretty. A good wife is faithful to her husband. She is intelligent, industrious, and creative. She is of great benefit to everyone around her including her husband, children and entire community. She knows her worth and speaks her mind but always in a way that builds her own good reputation and that of her husband. This woman lives an extraordinary life because she lives it for and before God.

My Reflections and Responses:

_____

_____

Date: _____   317

Ecclesiastes 1:3-4 *3 What's there to show for a lifetime of work, a lifetime of working your fingers to the bone? 4 One generation goes its way, the next one arrives, but nothing changes — it's business as usual for old planet earth.*

If your life is spent working hard to accomplish something here on earth, save your energy and avoid the disappointment; when the new generation arrives, the old one is soon forgotten and life goes on much the same. If your life is spent loving God and others, anything beyond that is a bonus. You've already fulfilled your purpose and received a reward; love is both.

My Reflections and Responses:

_____

_____

_____

_____

_____

_____

_____

_____

_____

_____

Date: _____   318

Ecclesiastes 1:5-7 *5 The sun comes up and the sun goes down, then does it again, and again — the same old round. 6 The wind blows south, the wind blows north. Around and around and around it blows, blowing this way, then that — the whirling, erratic wind. 7 All the rivers flow into the sea, but the sea never fills up. The rivers keep flowing to the same old place, and then start all over and do it again.*

There's a repetitious pattern to life on earth. The same things keep happening over and over again. If you just removed people from this planet, life would be very predictable; it would also be boring and monotonous. The infinite variety, countless surprises and extraordinary excitement yet to be discovered in this lifetime, on this planet, can be found primarily within relationships; relationship with God first and everyone else we encounter after that. Because no two people were created alike, no two relationships will ever be exactly alike; that's something to look forward to.

My Reflections and Responses:

_____

_____

_____

_____

_____

Date: _____

Ecclesiastes 1:8-10 *8 Everything's boring, utterly boring — no one can find any meaning in it. Boring to the eye, boring to the ear. 9 What was will be again, what happened will happen again. There's nothing new on this earth. Year after year it's the same old thing. 10 Does someone call out, "Hey, this is new"? Don't get excited — it's the same old story.*

If the same things keep happening over and over again, if, after all this time on earth, we've finally run out of new and different, there must be a purpose in all that repetition. There must be a reason we all go through much the same process from birth to death; something God wants each of us to experience before we move on. The seasons we all go through haven't outlived their usefulness or he would have moved on to something different. God created this planet and he made it predictable for a reason not yet fully understood. Is it possible, with everything around us remaining much the same day after day, year after year, generation after generation, that our real challenge lies within, not without?

My Reflections and Responses:

_____

_____

_____

_____

Ecclesiastes 1:11 *Nobody remembers what happened yesterday. And the things that will happen tomorrow? Nobody'll remember them either. Don't count on being remembered.*

If you count on being remembered, what you've done your short time here on earth was probably done for the wrong reason. It's not important that we be remembered; only that Jesus never be forgotten. It's not in this world but the next that we were created and intended to last forever; there, we can never be forgotten because we will always be present.

My Reflections and Responses:

_____

_____

_____

_____

_____

_____

_____

_____

_____

_____

_____

Date: _____

Ecclesiastes 1:12-14 *12 Call me "the Quester." I've been king over Israel in Jerusalem. 13 I looked most carefully into everything, searched out all that is done on this earth. And let me tell you, there's not much to write home about. God hasn't made it easy for us. 14 I've seen it all and it's nothing but smoke — smoke, and spitting into the wind.*

Solomon had the authority and the resources to check out everything here on earth and all that we would call real, he called smoke. The only thing that matters and has a chance of lasting is what we were made for in the first place; our relationship with God, his son Jesus and his Holy Spirit and our relationships with others to the degree that they reflect our relationship with Him.

My Reflections and Responses:

_____

_____

_____

_____

_____

_____

_____

_____

_____

_____

Date: _____

Ecclesiastes 1:16-17 *16 I said to myself, "I know more and I'm wiser than anyone before me in Jerusalem. I've stockpiled wisdom and knowledge." 17 What I've finally concluded is that so-called wisdom and knowledge are mindless and witless — nothing but spitting into the wind.*

The very one who told us to seek after wisdom and knowledge has concluded that they are of little or no use. Maybe seeking after these things, which can only be found in God, is where the real value lies, not in finding them. Compared to God's wisdom and knowledge, which is total and complete, what we could ever hope to accumulate during our short time on earth is pitiful, but if seeking points us in God's direction, and brings us closer to him, we've found something of immeasurable value and worth.

My Reflections and Responses:

_____

_____

_____

_____

_____

_____

_____

Date: _____   323

Ecclesiastes 1:18 *Much learning earns you much trouble. The more you know, the more you hurt.*

While it's true the more you know, the more you hurt, it's also true that the more you love, the greater chance you have of hurting, but God has put such a need to love and be loved inside of us that it's worth the hurt. To live out the life that Jesus called us to is not painless, but worth it. He has given us the capacity to endure the amount of pain necessary to accomplish the assignment he has given us. If you don't want extra pain, don't go where he hasn't sent you.

My Reflections and Responses:

_____

_____

_____

_____

_____

_____

_____

_____

_____

Date: _____

Ecclesiastes 2:2-3 *2 What do I think of the fun-filled life? Insane! Inane! My verdict on the pursuit of happiness? Who needs it? 3 With the help of a bottle of wine and all the wisdom I could muster, I tried my level best to penetrate the absurdity of life. I wanted to get a handle on anything useful we mortals might do during the years we spend on this earth.*

If life is all about pleasure, getting everything you want, doing whatever you feel like doing, Solomon should have been the happiest man to ever walk this earth. He's been there, done that, and gotten the t-shirt to prove it; his experiment in excess turned out to be a complete failure; he ended up hating life. You don't have to be as wise as Solomon to realize that he was looking for happiness in the wrong places. Maybe happiness isn't something ever to be found but something to be experienced as we peruse an ongoing relationship with our Lord.

My Reflections and Responses:

_____

_____

_____

_____

_____

_____

Date: _____   325

Ecclesiastes 2:9-11   *9 Oh, how I prospered! I left all my predecessors in Jerusalem far behind, left them behind in the dust. What's more, I kept a clear head through it all. 10 Everything I wanted I took — I never said no to myself. I gave in to every impulse, held back nothing. I sucked the marrow of pleasure out of every task — my reward to myself for a hard day's work! 11 Then I took a good look at everything I'd done, looked at all the sweat and hard work. But when I looked, I saw nothing but smoke. Smoke and spitting into the wind. There was nothing to any of it. Nothing.*

No matter how great your success, how wonderful your life, how extravagantly you indulge yourself, if your goal in life is to see how much you can get rather than how much you can give, you'll end up empty, lonely, discouraged and feeling that your life was a total waste. No matter how hard you try, you can never lift yourself up to greater heights; you can only offer and accept an extended hand.

My Reflections and Responses:

_____

_____

_____

_____

_____

_____

Date: _____   326

Ecclesiastes 2:12-14 *12 And then I took a hard look at what's smart and what's stupid. What's left to do after you've been king? That's a hard act to follow. You just do what you can, and that's it. 13 But I did see that it's better to be smart than stupid, just as light is better than darkness. 14 Even so, though the smart ones see where they're going and the stupid ones grope in the dark, they're all the same in the end. One fate for all — and that's it.*

Two men, starting out in the same place, travel to a distant city. The smart one takes the lighted path, able to see his way clearly, avoiding all obstacles that might have hindered him, and arrives safely at his destination. The stupid man takes the dark path. With no light to illuminate his way, he stumbles, trips, bumps into unseen obstacles, but eventually arrives at the exact same destination. Why does Solomon say that smart is better than stupid and light is better than dark if both end up the same place? The journey must be as important as the final destination, if not more.

My Reflections and Responses:

_____

_____

_____

_____

_____

Date: _____   327

Ecclesiastes 2:15-17 *15 When I realized that my fate's the same as the fool's, I had to ask myself, "So why bother being wise?" It's all smoke, nothing but smoke. 16 The smart and the stupid both disappear out of sight. In a day or two they're both forgotten. Yes, both the smart and the stupid die, and that's it. 17 I hate life. As far as I can see, what happens on earth is a bad business. It's smoke — and spitting into the wind.*

If celebrity and fame are what you're looking for; if being remembered forever is the reward you most value, save your time and effort; when you're out of sight, you'll most likely be out of mind, if not immediately, certainly within a generation or two. If you've accumulated treasures in heaven, and what you most treasure here on earth are your relationships with God and others, you'll consider your life worthwhile, and you'll have gotten all the good there is to get out of your short stay here in these temporary quarters.

My Reflections and Responses:

_____

_____

_____

_____

_____

_____

Date: _____   328

Ecclesiastes 2:18-19 18 And I hated everything I'd accomplished and accumulated on this earth. I can't take it with me — no, I have to leave it to whoever comes after me. 19 Whether they're worthy or worthless — and who's to tell? — they'll take over the earthly results of my intense thinking and hard work. Smoke.

Solomon was so right when he called his accom-plishments and accumulations, intense thinking and hard work here on earth, smoke. Why he cared what happened to them, and who ended up with them after he was gone, is what I don't understand. He must have forgotten that it was his spirit, not his stuff that was built to last forever. I'm pretty sure, when he reached his eternity with the Lord; he got a good laugh out of all that fretting over nothing but smoke.

My Reflections and Responses:

_____

_____

_____

_____

_____

_____

_____

Date: _____

Ecclesiastes 2:20-23 20 That's when I called it quits, gave up on anything that could be hoped for on this earth. 21 What's the point of working your fingers to the bone if you hand over what you worked for to someone who never lifted a finger for it? Smoke, that's what it is. A bad business from start to finish. 22 So what do you get from a life of hard labor? 23 Pain and grief from dawn to dusk. Never a decent night's rest. Nothing but smoke.

It's about time we all call it quits and give up on anything that could be hoped for on this earth. Our hope has never been in this world. Nothing we accomplish here is going to last anyway. That doesn't mean we should call it quits on life. Life was created to last forever; a short time here on this earth and then forever with our Lord. Work your fingers to the bone if you like, it's optional; love like your life depends on it, it does if you want that life that lasts forever.

My Reflections and Responses:

_____

_____

_____

_____

_____

_____

Date: _____   330

Ecclesiastes 3:1-8 *1 There's an opportune time to do things, a right time for everything on the earth: 2 A right time for birth and another for death, a right time to plant and another to reap, 3 A right time to kill and another to heal, a right time to destroy and another to construct, 4 A right time to cry and another to laugh, a right time to lament and another to cheer, 5 A right time to make love and another to abstain, a right time to embrace and another to part, 6 A right time to search and another to count your losses, a right time to hold on and another to let go, 7 A right time to rip out and another to mend, a right time to shut up and another to speak up, 8 A right time to love and another to hate, a right time to wage war and another to make peace.*

How do you know when the right time is? Sometimes the "right time" is dictated by the seasons; you don't plant in the dead of winter. Sometimes the circumstance makes the "right time" obvious; you don't cheer a tragedy, you lament it. More often the "right time" isn't so apparent. That's when you need to be intimately in touch with the heart and mind of Jesus. He asks us in Matthew 11:29 to walk with him, work with him, watch how he does it and "learn the unforced rhythms of grace"; that's how you'll always know just the right time to do exactly the right thing.

My Reflections and Responses:

_____

_____

Date: _____

Ecclesiastes 3:9-13 *9 But in the end, does it really make a difference what anyone does? 10 I've had a good look at what God has given us to do — busywork, mostly. 11 True, God made everything beautiful in itself and in its time — but he's left us in the dark, so we can never know what God is up to, whether he's coming or going. 12 I've decided that there's nothing better to do than go ahead and have a good time and get the most we can out of life. 13 That's it — eat, drink, and make the most of your job. It's God's gift.*

Does it really make a difference what anyone does? The answer is yes. All work seems like busywork if we don't know its purpose and God doesn't feel compelled to fill us in on every detail. He gave us faith to fill in the blanks and answer the unanswered questions. It's true that we seldom know what God's up to, but whether he's coming or going, he's always present through his Holy Spirit. There's nothing wrong with having a good time, enjoying life and making the most of our jobs; God loves us and wants us to benefit from the earth that he created especially for us. But in the end, it really does matter what we do if we do it for him because we love him. Solomon eventually figured that out.

My Reflections and Responses:

_____

_____

_____

Date: _____

Ecclesiastes 3:19-22 *19 Humans and animals come to the same end — humans die, animals die. We all breathe the same air. So there's really no advantage in being human. None. Everything's smoke. 20 We all end up in the same place — we all came from dust, we all end up as dust. 21 Nobody knows for sure that the human spirit rises to heaven or that the animal spirit sinks into the earth. 22 So I made up my mind that there's nothing better for us men and women than to have a good time in whatever we do — that's our lot...*

If there were no god, there really would be no advantage in being human; actually, there's a big disadvantage. Animals don't bother with a conscience. They don't make plans for retirement. There are no laws to break or obey. Instinct tells them all they need to know about life; when to go to sleep, when to get up, when to mate and what to eat. There is no free will to worry about because there are no real choices. Life would be so much easier if we were just animals. But there is God, and he made us in his image to rule and rein and live forever with him. Being like him will never be as easy as being animal but look at what we get; choice, freedom, understanding, relationship, future, awareness, and a thousand other perks, but most of all we get to love and be loved by our Father and by his family, forever.

My Reflections and Responses:

_____

_____

Date: _____   333

Ecclesiastes 4:1-3 *1 Next I turned my attention to all the outrageous violence that takes place on this planet — the tears of the victims, no one to comfort them; the iron grip of oppressors, no one to rescue the victims from them. 2 So I congratulated the dead who are already dead instead of the living who are still alive. 3 But luckier than the dead or the living is the person who has never even been, who has never seen the bad business that takes place on this earth.*

King Solomon was temporarily stuck right in the middle of the human story. He was forgetting the beginning, and hadn't yet read the back of the book where Jesus rescues us from the outrageous violence and incredible wickedness that occurs when men forget about God and become more like animals than like their creator. It's only through the eyes of faith that we can see beyond the dismal present to our glorious forever. The "never born" get to avoid the "bad business" that takes place on this earth but they also have no future, have no forever and have no Lord.

My Reflections and Responses:

_____

_____

_____

_____

_____

Date: _____   334

Ecclesiastes 4:9-10 *4 It's better to have a partner than go it alone. Share the work, share the wealth. 10 And if one falls down, the other helps, but if there's no one to help, tough!*

When God made Eve he was acknowledging this truth. Adam had plenty of animals but without Eve, he couldn't find a suitable partner. Someone made in God's image could never partner with someone who wasn't.

My Reflections and Responses:

_____

_____

_____

_____

_____

_____

_____

_____

_____

_____

_____

Date: _____   335

Ecclesiastes 4:11 *Two in a bed warm each other. Alone, you shiver all night.*

We were not created to be independent but interdependent. As wonderful and exquisite as Adam's relationship was with God, he needed Eve to keep him warm at night.

My Reflections and Responses:

_____

_____

_____

_____

_____

_____

_____

_____

_____

_____

_____

_____

Date: _____

Ecclesiastes 4:12 *By yourself you're unprotected. With a friend you can face the worst. Can you round up a third? A three-stranded rope isn't easily snapped.*

A three-stranded rope isn't three strands lying next to each other; it's three strands intertwined. Strength comes out of the relationship with each other, not the close proximity to each other.

My Reflections and Responses:

_____

_____

_____

_____

_____

_____

_____

_____

_____

_____

_____

_____

Date: _____

Ecclesiastes 5:2 *Don't shoot off your mouth, or speak before you think. Don't be too quick to tell God what you think he wants to hear. God's in charge, not you — the less you speak, the better.*

When you tell anyone what you think they want to hear, you're trying to trick them into believing you agree with them. Do you really think God can be fooled by such shenanigans? The more you speak, the less time you have to listen. When you're in a conversation with the one who knows all and created all, you might want to spend more time listening than speaking.

My Reflections and Responses:

_____

_____

_____

_____

_____

_____

_____

_____

_____

Date: _____

Ecclesiastes 5:3 Over-work makes for restless sleep. Over-talk shows you up as a fool.

Over-anything is too much of a good thing. If there's a time for everything, there's also "not the right time" for everything. Time and timing seem to be as important as what you're timing.

My Reflections and Responses:

_____

_____

_____

_____

_____

_____

_____

_____

_____

_____

_____

Date: _____

Ecclesiastes 5:4-5 *4 When you tell God you'll do something, do it — now. God takes no pleasure in foolish gabble. Vow it, then do it. 5 Far better not to vow in the first place than to vow and not pay up.*

It's better to do than to promise. A promise or vow is a debt to be paid at a later date. If you are slow to pay your debts or don't pay them at all, who is going to be willing to offer you credit the next time? Don't use a credit card if you can pay cash. Don't promise if you can just do it now.

My Reflections and Responses:

_____

_____

_____

_____

_____

_____

_____

_____

_____

_____

Date: _____   340

Ecclesiastes 5:8-9 *8 Don't be too upset when you see the poor kicked around, and justice and right violated all over the place. Exploitation filters down from one petty official to another. There's no end to it, and nothing can be done about it. 9 But the good earth doesn't cheat anyone — even a bad king is honestly served by a field.*

Don't get so busy chasing every injustice that you forget to sow good seed and encourage others to do the same. At harvest time, the good and the bad will be easy to separate. If you don't sow good seed because others might be sowing bad, there will be nothing good to reap at harvest time. If, while you're busy sowing good seed, you can right a wrong, do it, but remember your main focus should be on the good, not the bad.

My Reflections and Responses:

_____

_____

_____

_____

_____

_____

_____

_____

_____

Date: _____   341

Ecclesiastes 5:10-11 *10 The one who loves money is never satisfied with money, Nor the one who loves wealth with big profits. More smoke. 11 The more loot you get, the more looters show up. And what fun is that — to be robbed in broad daylight?*

If you love and horde what can be stolen, eventually it will be. If you spend your money doing good, there's no money left to steal; the thief isn't interested in stealing good, and you've gotten and given full value for your money, here and in heaven. If you love what can't be stolen, relationships, generosity, self-sacrifice, and all of the fruits of the Spirit, you won't have to stay up all night guarding your treasure.

My Reflections and Responses:

_____

_____

_____

_____

_____

_____

_____

_____

Date: _____

Ecclesiastes 5:13-17 *13 Here's a piece of bad luck I've seen happen: A man hoards far more wealth than is good for him 14 And then loses it all in a bad business deal. He fathered a child but hasn't a cent left to give him. 15 He arrived naked from the womb of his mother; He'll leave in the same condition — with nothing. 16 This is bad luck, for sure — naked he came, naked he went. So what was the point of working for a salary of smoke? 17 All for a miserable life spent in the dark?*

Another man arrives naked in this world, works hard, lives right and loves extravagantly. He fathers a child, raises him with the same values he has lived by all of his life and leaves this world naked but with the love of family, friends and a community that will be glad to look after his child when he's gone. He has left his child with the strength of character to carry on and add to his good name; a far more valuable inheritance than a few coins that could be lost in one bad business deal.

My Reflections and Responses:

_____

_____

_____

_____

_____

Date: _____

Ecclesiastes 5:18-20 *18 After looking at the way things are on this earth, here's what I've decided is the best way to live: Take care of yourself, have a good time, and make the most of whatever job you have for as long as God gives you life. And that's about it. That's the human lot. 19 Yes, we should make the most of what God gives, both the bounty and the capacity to enjoy it, accepting what's given and delighting in the work. It's God's gift! 20 God deals out joy in the present, the now. It's useless to brood over how long we might live.*

The key to living the way Solomon suggests is delighting in the work. We were all created with a need to work or contribute. We either work for God or we're working against him. If we accept, enjoy and delight in the work he has given us to do, we'll have plenty of hard times, plenty of good times, live full and fulfilling lives, and be far too busy to worry about how long we live or how soon we might die.

My Reflections and Responses:

_____

_____

_____

_____

_____

_____

Date: _____   344

Ecclesiastes 6:6 *Even if someone lived a thousand years —* *make it two thousand! — but didn't enjoy anything, what's* *the point? Doesn't everyone end up in the same place?*

There are some things that just don't go together; if you want one, you have to give up the other. To enjoy your life, whether it's ten, a hundred or a thousand years long, there are some things you simply have to let go of. You won't be happy if you hang on to anger. You can never feel satisfied and be stingy at the same time. You can't live a life of love and hold on to hatred in your heart. You have to decide what you want most because you can't have it all; but then, who would want to?

My Reflections and Responses:

_____

_____

_____

_____

_____

_____

_____

_____

Date: _____   345

Ecclesiastes 7:1 *A good reputation is better than a fat bank account. Your death date tells more than your birth date.*

On the day you were born, you had no reputation. Your gender, height and weight were the first and only entries in your book; everything else would be written as you took what you were born with, added what you were taught, and blended them, along with your own free will, into a unique existence unlike any other before or after. On the day you die your story will have been written; no more rewrites, additions or deletions. If it's a story worth telling, many future generations will hear and be inspired by it; if not, your children will burn through your fat bank account, try to live down your bad reputation, and forget you as quickly as they can.

My Reflections and Responses:

_____

_____

_____

_____

_____

_____

_____

Date: _____   346

Ecclesiastes 7:5 You'll get more from the rebuke of a sage than from the song and dance of fools.

Be a sage. Realize how valuable your rebukes are and use them wisely. If you use them for your own gain or to harshly attack those you disagree with, they'll be wasted and most likely rejected. If you deliver them with love and kindness, even though they might sting, they will enrich and instruct their recipients and you will have made an important contribution to their lives.

My Reflections and Responses:

_____

_____

_____

_____

_____

_____

_____

_____

_____

_____

Date: _____   347

Ecclesiastes 7:9 Don't be quick to fly off the handle. Anger boomerangs. You can spot a fool by the lumps on his head.

If you go around angry all the time, eventually someone bigger, tougher and angrier then you is bound to take offense. If you start collecting more than the usual number of lumps on your head, you might want to examine your attitude. If you get the occasional lump now and then, it's probably just the cost of being a Christian; don't make too much of it.

My Reflections and Responses:

_____

_____

_____

_____

_____

_____

_____

_____

_____

_____

_____

Date: _____   348

Ecclesiastes 7:11-12 *11 Wisdom is better when it's paired with money, Especially if you get both while you're still living. 12 Double protection: wisdom and wealth! Plus this bonus: Wisdom energizes its owner.*

If you have to choose one, go with wisdom, but don't despise money; look at it as your distribution system. With money, you can share your wisdom with many more people and you will have the means to do what wisdom tells you to do for others. If you're living for the Lord, you know you got your money from the same place you got your wisdom; if not, you're not very wise, and your money won't do you much good anyway.

My Reflections and Responses:

_____

_____

_____

_____

_____

_____

_____

_____

_____

Date: _____   349

Ecclesiastes 7:14 On a good day, enjoy yourself; On a bad day, examine your conscience. God arranges for both kinds of days so that we won't take anything for granted.

E very day is God's day and is given to you for a reason; some go better than others and some feel better than others but yours is a walk of faith not feelings. He is with you in good times and bad, uphill or down, rain or shine. Get up each morning and look forward to a God day, not just a good day.

My Reflections and Responses:

_____

_____

_____

_____

_____

_____

_____

_____

_____

_____

_____

Date: _____

Ecclesiastes 7:15-17 *15 I've seen it all in my brief and pointless life — here a good person cut down in the middle of doing good, there a bad person living a long life of sheer evil. 16 So don't knock yourself out being good, and don't go overboard being wise. Believe me, you won't get anything out of it. 17 But don't press your luck by being bad, either. And don't be reckless. Why die needlessly?*

If the wisest man on earth called his a brief and pointless life, I wouldn't advise you to put too much effort into making a name for yourself, either as the best or the worst. Be content with living out the life that God laid out for you. If that involves wealth or fame, don't be too impressed; just use it for his glory. If yours is a life of obscurity, don't be too disappointed, he still has a unique reason for your existence; find it, do it and your reward will be great, even if your life didn't appear to be.

My Reflections and Responses:

_____

_____

_____

_____

_____

_____

Date: _____   351

Ecclesiastes 7:21-22 21 Don't eavesdrop on the conversation of others. What if the gossip's about you and you'd rather not hear it? 22 You've done that a few times, haven't you — said things behind someone's back you wouldn't say to his face?

If God wanted everyone to know the private thoughts and conversations of others, he could have easily created us with that ability but he didn't. Even if your goal is to live a transparent life, you build your bathroom and bedroom with walls, not windows. Some things are meant to stay private. On the other hand, be careful to speak the truth, even behind closed doors; a window might be open and someone might be listening.

My Reflections and Responses:

_____

_____

_____

_____

_____

_____

_____

_____

_____

_____

Date: _____   352

Ecclesiastes 7:26-29 *26 One discovery: A woman can be a bitter pill to swallow, full of seductive scheming and grasping. The lucky escape her; the undiscerning get caught. 27 At least this is my experience — what I, the Quester, have pieced together as I've tried to make sense of life. 28 But the wisdom I've looked for I haven't found. I didn't find one man or woman in a thousand worth my while. 29 Yet I did spot one ray of light in this murk: God made men and women true and upright; we're the ones who've made a mess of things.*

Solomon didn't say no one was worth his while; just that they are rare and hard to find. Be the rare one who has remained true and upright; look for and be the one in a thousand or one in ten thousand if that's what it takes. You haven't found the right mate until both of you feel fortunate and blessed.

My Reflections and Responses:

_____

_____

_____

_____

_____

_____

_____

_____

Date: _____   353

Ecclesiastes 8:1 *There's nothing better than being wise, knowing how to interpret the meaning of life. Wisdom puts light in the eyes, and gives gentleness to words and manners.*

Being wise is not the same as being a know-it-all. It's not just an accumulation of knowledge that makes one wise; it's the application, the method of delivery and the timing that takes a person beyond smart to wise. If you want a chance to share what God has shown you, be a pleasant container for all that wisdom.

My Reflections and Responses:

_____

_____

_____

_____

_____

_____

_____

_____

_____

_____

_____

Date: _____   354

Ecclesiastes 8:6-7 6 *Yes, there's a right time and way for everything, even though, unfortunately, we miss it for the most part. 7 It's true that no one knows what's going to happen, or when. Who's around to tell us?*

Solomon had a disadvantage that we don't have to live with. Jesus hadn't come, gone and sent his Holy Spirit to live in us and be our constant companion. Now we do have someone around to tell us the right time and way if we'll only listen.

My Reflections and Responses:

_____

_____

_____

_____

_____

_____

_____

_____

_____

_____

_____

Date: _____

Ecclesiastes 8:11 *Because the sentence against evil deeds is so long in coming, people in general think they can get by with murder.*

I f punishment was a good deterrent, no one would ever go to jail twice but we know that prisons are full of second, third and fourth timers. If even long or harsh sentences can't stop people from their evil deeds, what will? Neither punishment nor reward is sufficient motivation but love is. If your reason for living right and doing good is because you love God, others and yourself, you create a perpetual motion machine. The more you love, the greater your capacity and the stronger your desire to love becomes. Eventually you gain enough momentum that nothing can stop you.

My Reflections and Responses:

_____

_____

_____

_____

_____

_____

_____

_____

Date: _____   356

Ecclesiastes 8:12-13 *12 Even though a person sins and gets by with it hundreds of times throughout a long life, I'm still convinced that the good life is reserved for the person who fears God, who lives reverently in his presence, 13 and that the evil person will not experience a "good" life. No matter how many days he lives, they'll all be as flat and colorless as a shadow — because he doesn't fear God.*

What is the "good life"? If it's indulging in every pleasure known to man, evil will get you there quicker than reverence. If it's going after what feels good, rather than what is good, fear of God won't be of much help. If by "good life" you mean a fulfilling one, with plenty of love, satisfying relationships, significant contributions and a good foundation and reputation to pass on to future generations, you'll only find that kind of life in His presence. Only those who fear God will ever really get to know God and experience a life lived in his presence.

My Reflections and Responses:

_____

_____

_____

_____

_____

_____

Date: _____   357

Ecclesiastes 8:14-15 14 Here's something that happens all the time and makes no sense at all: Good people get what's coming to the wicked, and bad people get what's coming to the good. I tell you, this makes no sense. It's smoke. 15 So, I'm all for just going ahead and having a good time — the best possible. The only earthly good men and women can look forward to is to eat and drink well and have a good time — compensation for the struggle for survival these few years God gives us on earth.

A life of faith is not a life of instant gratification but of deep satisfaction. If you're looking for immediate reward for the good people and punishment for the bad, you're undoubtedly assuming that you're one of the good ones and wandering where your reward is. First, no one will ever be good enough; any reward we get was earned by Jesus and given as a pure gift. Secondly, a life lived with him, and eternity spent in his presence, is the ultimate compensation for the small inconveniences we suffer during the few years spent here on earth. Finally, it's not up to us to determine who gets what, when; only to trust that God is a just God and better yet, a merciful one, and as his children, we will always get better than we deserve and more than we expect.

My Reflections and Responses:

_____

_____

Date: _____   358

Ecclesiastes 8:16-17 *16 When I determined to load up on wisdom and examine everything taking place on earth, I realized that if you keep your eyes open day and night without even blinking, 17 you'll still never figure out the meaning of what God is doing on this earth. Search as hard as you like, you're not going to make sense of it. No matter how smart you are, you won't get to the bottom of it.*

Thankfully, wisdom doesn't require that you know everything, only that you know what to do with what you do know. As the created, we can never hope to, nor do we need to understand the creator to benefit from his total understanding of us. We are far too wonderfully made and intricately designed, to expect to be able to figure everything out. That doesn't mean we should ever stop pushing the limits of our knowledge. Part of his design and pleasure was to make us inquisitive and adventurous.

My Reflections and Responses:

_____

_____

_____

_____

_____

_____

Date: _____   359

Ecclesiastes 9:1-3 1 Anything's possible. 2 It's one fate for everybody — righteous and wicked, good people, bad people, the nice and the nasty, worshipers and non-worshipers, committed and uncommitted. 3 I find this outrageous — the worst thing about living on this earth — that everyone's lumped together in one fate. Is it any wonder that so many people are obsessed with evil? Is it any wonder that people go crazy right and left? Life leads to death. That's it.

No one escapes death; everyone passes through that same door. If it doesn't matter how you get there, and it doesn't matter where you go from there, what's the point; it would be better to skip the whole thing. If you believe life well lived on earth matters, even if it doesn't allow you to avoid death, and if you believe in the hereafter, then life doesn't lead to or end in death; it takes you through death on your way to eternity with or without God. The life you live here and the choices you make now determine how that eternity will be spent; that's not outrageous, that's incredible.

My Reflections and Responses:

_____

_____

_____

_____

Date: _____   360

Ecclesiastes 9:4-6   *4 Still, anyone selected out for life has hope, for, as they say, "A living dog is better than a dead lion." 5 The living at least know something, even if it's only that they're going to die. But the dead know nothing and get nothing. They're a minus that no one remembers. 6 Their loves, their hates, yes, even their dreams, are long gone. There's not a trace of them left in the affairs of this earth.*

Solomon, with the wealth and power to indulge himself with every pleasure known to man, often found it difficult to find a good reason to go on living, but even he concluded that life is better than death; not easer but definitely better. If this world was all we had to look forward to, there are days when it might seem better not to have been born, but there are other days that more than make up for those difficult ones, and there is something even better to hope for and look forward to after we're gone from this world. As for not remembering the dead, look whose life and words we still study and quote after all this time. If you want to be remembered, do something memorable; Solomon did and he still is.

My Reflections and Responses:

_____

_____

_____

_____

Date: _____

Ecclesiastes 9:7-10 *7 Seize life! Eat bread with gusto, drink wine with a robust heart. Oh yes — God takes pleasure in your pleasure! 8 Dress festively every morning. Don't skimp on colors and scarves. 9 Relish life with the spouse you love each and every day of your precarious life. Each day is God's gift. It's all you get in exchange for the hard work of staying alive. Make the most of each one! 10 Whatever turns up, grab it and do it. And heartily! This is your last and only chance at it, for there's neither work to do nor thoughts to think in the company of the dead, where you're most certainly headed.*

L ive and enjoy each day as though it was your last, it might be; live each one as though you were going to be around to explain it to your great-grandchildren, you might last longer than you think. It's the balance than prevents you from putting off until you never get around to doing what's most important, but causes you to consider the impact your actions will have on yours and your family's future. To achieve that balance, you'll first need to determine what is most important to you. You might start with a list.

My Reflections and Responses:

_____

_____

_____

_____

_____

Ecclesiastes 9:11-12 11 The race is not always to the swift, nor the battle to the strong, nor satisfaction to the wise, nor riches to the smart, nor grace to the learned. Sooner or later bad luck hits us all. 12 No one can predict misfortune. Like fish caught in a cruel net or birds in a trap, so men and women are caught.

It's good to prepare for any eventuality with education, exercise and training; you'll be much better equipped to cope with catastrophe than those who are unprepared, and it gives you the advantage in good times as well. Just don't be surprised when you face disaster of a magnitude totally beyond your abilities and resources. Everyone eventually does. That's when you really begin to understand your need for God. If you could make it on your own, you should; you can't, so don't waist precious time trying. Turn quickly to the one who is never caught off guard or taken by surprise; the one who is always more than sufficient in every situation, your heavenly father.

My Reflections and Responses:

_____

_____

_____

_____

_____

Date: _____   363

Ecclesiastes 9:17-18 *17 The quiet words of the wise are more effective than the ranting of a king of fools. 18 Wisdom is better than warheads, but one hothead can ruin the good earth.*

How prophetic. If you're relying on government to be your ultimate protection, be very afraid. In this modern day nuclear world, one hothead can literally ruin the good earth. Thank God for God. Governments, and even governmental hotheads, operate with his permission and indulgence but never to the point of destroying this earth. He has his own plan for the end of this world and the rescue of all his children, at a time known only to him. In the meantime, do what you can to be a peacemaker, but put your hope for eternal peace in his hands.

My Reflections and Responses:

_____

_____

_____

_____

_____

_____

_____

Date: _____   364

Ecclesiastes 10:8 *Caution: The trap you set might catch you.*
Warning: Your accomplice in crime might double-cross you.

If you set a trap, you have to keep coming back to see what you've caught; eventually you might even catch yourself. How are you ever going to get ahead if you keep coming back to where you started? Just keep moving forward, no traps, no tricks. If you're trying to take advantage of someone else, do you really think your partner in crime will hesitate to take advantage of you if he gets the chance? You know you'd do the same to him.

My Reflections and Responses:

_____

_____

_____

_____

_____

_____

_____

_____

_____

Date: _____   365

Ecclesiastes 10:10 Remember: The duller the ax the harder the work; Use your head: the more brains, the less muscle.

God didn't put us over all the animals of the earth because we are stronger; many animals are stronger, bigger and a lot tougher. He made us smarter. Jesus said "I won't lay anything heavy or ill-fitting on you. Keep company with me and you'll learn to live freely and lightly." The work he intends for you to do doesn't take a lot of muscle but he does expect you to put that incredible brain he gave you to good use.

My Reflections and Responses:

_____

_____

_____

_____

_____

_____

_____

_____

_____

_____

Date: _____   366

Ecclesiastes 11:1-2 *1 Be generous: Invest in acts of charity. Charity yields high returns. 2 Don't hoard your goods; spread them around. Be a blessing to others. This could be your last night.*

The moment you give something away you have insured it against loss, theft, wear and tear. The value you receive from giving a gift never depreciates as long as you live, and is a treasure stored in heaven for eternity. Your last day on earth is your final opportunity to make this kind of investment, so don't wait till it's too late.

My Reflections and Responses:

_____

_____

_____

_____

_____

_____

_____

_____

_____

_____

Date: _____

Ecclesiastes 11:6 *Go to work in the morning and stick to it until evening without watching the clock. You never know from moment to moment how your work will turn out in the end.*

Your work is the job God has given you to do today. He might give you something you like better tomorrow, but don't be in a hurry to stop serving him today. If you do everything as to the Lord, you'll want to do your very best. If it's not something you would do for him, maybe you should stop doing it altogether.

My Reflections and Responses:

_____

_____

_____

_____

_____

_____

_____

_____

_____

_____

Date: _____   368

Ecclesiastes 11:7-8 *7 Oh, how sweet the light of day, and how wonderful to live in the sunshine! 8 Even if you live a long time, don't take a single day for granted. Take delight in each light-filled hour, remembering that there will also be many dark days and that most of what comes your way is smoke.*

If you took a photograph with no contrast, it would be completely white or totally black. Contrast allows you to see and enjoy the extremes and everything in-between. If there were no dark days, what would you compare a sunny day to; it wouldn't be sweet or wonderful, just another day. Don't despise your life in difficult times, even if you hate what's happening; its still life, which in itself is wonderful, you never have to go through it alone, and you will appreciate the good times even more.

My Reflections and Responses:

_____

_____

_____

_____

_____

_____

_____

_____

Date: _____   369

Ecclesiastes 11:9 You who are young, make the most of your youth. Relish your youthful vigor. Follow the impulses of your heart. If something looks good to you, pursue it. But know also that not just anything goes; you have to answer to God for every last bit of it.

When you're young, you have energy to spare. It's good to spend it chasing your dreams, even those that never amount to anything; how will you ever know if you don't try. In later life you'll have to conserve your energy because you'll have much less of it, but for now, take advantage of your surplus and peruse the improbable. Just remember there's still right and wrong, good and bad; youth doesn't exempt you from personal responsibility.

My Reflections and Responses:

_____

_____

_____

_____

_____

_____

_____

_____

Date: _____

Ecclesiastes 12:1-2 *1 Honor and enjoy your Creator while you're still young, before the years take their toll and your vigor wanes, 2 before your vision dims and the world blurs and the winter years keep you close to the fire.*

M ost old people wouldn't trade the knowledge and wisdom they've gained over the years for the vigor of youth, but if they could have both, they'd take them in a second. Don't waste your youth acting old before your time. Enjoy the extravagant energy God has given you for a short time to dream the incredible, hope for the improbable and peruse the impossible. When you're old and worn out, you'll have wonderful memories and exciting stories to tell your grandchildren of those youthful escapades; the great successes and even the monumental flops.

My Reflections and Responses:

_____

_____

_____

_____

_____

_____

_____

Date: _____

Ecclesiastes 12:3-8 *3 In old age, your body no longer serves you so well. Muscles slacken, grip weakens, joints stiffen. The shades are pulled down on the world. 4 You can't come and go at will. Things grind to a halt. The hum of the household fades away. You are wakened now by bird-song. 5 Hikes to the mountains are a thing of the past. Even a stroll down the road has its terrors. Your hair turns apple-blossom white, adorning a fragile and impotent matchstick body. Yes, you're well on your way to eternal rest, while your friends make plans for your funeral. 6 Life, lovely while it lasts, is soon over. Life as we know it, precious and beautiful, ends. 7 The body is put back in the same ground it came from. The spirit returns to God, who first breathed it. 8 It's all smoke, nothing but smoke. The Quester says that everything's smoke.*

It all seems pretty dismal. If it weren't for that one reality "The spirit returns to God" it might seem to be a sad commentary on our earthly existence. Fortunately for us, our bodies were designed to last for a little while and then ware out, freeing our eternal spirit to move on to our heavenly destination. Imagine being stuck in our earthly bodies for eternity; thank God it's all smoke. If it wasn't, look what we would be missing out on.

My Reflections and Responses:

_____

_____

_____

_____

Date: _____   372

Ecclesiastes 12:11 *The words of the wise prod us to live well. They're like nails hammered home, holding life together. They are given by God, the one Shepherd.*

The words of the wise are not just superior opinions expressed by superior individuals. If they are truly wise, their wisdom and their words come from the source of all wisdom, God. Whatever your gifts, wisdom, knowledge, healing, prophecy or something equally wonderful, remember they are gifts not wages; they are freely given to share with others and magnify the Lord. Enjoy them but use them wisely and reverently.

My Reflections and Responses:

_____

_____

_____

_____

_____

_____

_____

_____

_____

Date: _____ 373

Ecclesiastes 12:12-14 *12 But regarding anything beyond this, dear friend, go easy. There's no end to the publishing of books, and constant study wears you out so you're no good for anything else. 13 The last and final word is this: Fear God. Do what he tells you. 14 And that's it. Eventually God will bring everything that we do out into the open and judge it according to its hidden intent, whether it's good or evil.*

Don't give yourself a headache memorizing every new book that comes out claiming to unlock the mysteries of God and the universe. Life can be hard enough without making it more difficult than it needs to be. The truth is usually quite simple and straightforward. Respect, revere and obey God and trust that your Lord Jesus will cover your failures. If you stick with that, at the end of days, when God reveals all, you won't have anything to worry about.

My Reflections and Responses:

_____

_____

_____

_____

_____

_____

_____

Date: _____   374

Notes:

375

Notes:

Notes:

Notes:

Notes:

_____

_____

_____

_____

_____

_____

_____

_____

_____

_____

_____

_____

_____

_____

_____

_____

_____

Notes:

Notes:

MorningWhispersOnline.com

Visit us online to find out more about:

- Morning Whispers: Book Two
- Ordering Morning Whispers
- Contacting the author
- David Morgan, Author & Therapist
- Much more

CompassCounseling.com

CPSIA information can be obtained
at www.ICGtesting.com
Printed in the USA
FSHW010916271018
53349FS